# WELL
# DONE

# WELL
# DONE

*a faithful worker with a missionary heart*

## LILA LEE MOORE COX

This book is a work of non-fiction. Unless otherwise noted, the author and the publisher make no explicit guarantees as to the accuracy of the information contained in this book and in some cases, names of people and places have been altered to protect their privacy.

Archway Publishing books may be ordered through booksellers or by contacting:

Archway Publishing
1663 Liberty Drive
Bloomington, IN 47403
www.archwaypublishing.com
844-669-3957

Because of the dynamic nature of the Internet, any web addresses or links contained in this book may have changed since publication and may no longer be valid. The views expressed in this work are solely those of the author and do not necessarily reflect the views of the publisher, and the publisher hereby disclaims any responsibility for them.

Any people depicted in stock imagery provided by Getty Images are models, and such images are being used for illustrative purposes only. Certain stock imagery © Getty Images.

Unless otherwise noted, all Scripture quotations are taken from the ESV® Bible (The Holy Bible, English Standard Version®), copyright © 2001 by Crossway, a publishing ministry of Good News Publishers. Used by permission. All rights reserved.

Scripture quotation marked AMP is taken from the Amplified® Version, Copyright © 2015 by The Lockman Foundation. Used by permission.

ISBN: 978-1-6657-6832-0 (sc)
ISBN: 978-1-6657-6831-3 (e)

Library of Congress Control Number: 2024923675

Print information available on the last page.

Archway Publishing rev. date: 12/11/2024

*… and what does the Lord require of you*
*but to do justice, and to love kindness,*
*and to walk humbly with your God?*
*Micah 6:8 ESV*

# CONTENTS

*"For everything there is a season, and a time*
*for every matter under heaven:*
*a time to be born, and a time to die;*
*a time to plant, and a time to pluck up what is planted,"*

*Ecclesiastes 3:1-2*

# SOMEWHERE SOMEDAY

## 1929 – 1939

God brought me into this world on April 4, 1929, at 4 a.m. in Lake City, Florida into the home of my parents, May Love Aldrich Moore and James Augustus Moore, their third child. My siblings were a brother, James Arad Moore, born June 21, 1926, in Jacksonville, Florida and a sister, Nellie Claire Moore, born September 19, 1927, in St. Petersburg, Florida.

At the time of my birth, both Arad and Nellie were gravely ill suffering with colitis. I was thirteen days old when Arad died at the tender age two years and ten months. Nellie was near death herself so they kept Arad's body two additional days expecting Nellie would join him and they could be buried together.

My parents were grief stricken to the point that my fraternal grandmother, Charlotte Adele Flynt Moore took me to Jacksonville and cared for me until I was five months old. May Love and James could no longer bear to live in the house where Arad had died and it was heartbreaking watching Nellie, who had rebounded from illness, search for Arad calling his name, and too young to understand why her constant companion and playmate didn't appear when she desperately cried for him. The Great Depression had begun. Reunited with my parents and sister, we moved to Miami where my dad found work in a paint and body shop. Daddy's big steady hands could paint freehand the pinstripes on the cars very popular those days.

A failed pregnancy and near fatal miscarriage happened before their fourth child, Thelma Adele, was born November 22, 1932. Mama was deeply disappointed that her baby was not born a boy, having lost her only son. Daddy would encourage her to look at her beautiful daughter and bond with her, but another daughter didn't begin to fill the hole left in her heart.

I'm sure this impacted Nellie as she vowed at age seven to never marry and never have a man tell her what to do. And true to her word, Nellie never married.

*There's a lot of miles between today and someday.*

We soon moved from the house where Thelma Adele was born on N.E. 69th Street to a house on 10th Avenue very near the Seaboard Railway Station. Thus began my life-long love affair with trains. I would lie awake at night just to listen to the trains arriving and leaving the station wanting so much to board one. Dreaming of going "somewhere" I would think about faraway places. Believing that someday I will travel the world. Singing "Somewhere Over the Rainbow" solidified my desire to be somewhere else – somewhere new and exciting. Of course, at this age I didn't know all that God would let me see included the perfect circle of a rainbow.

> *You make known to me the path of life,*
> *in your presence there is fullness of joy;*
> *at your hand are pleasures forevermore.*
> *Psalm 16:11*

We were still living by my trains on 10th Avenue when I began school at age six – Santa Clara Elementary School. Before my first year of school ended, we moved again. This time to 1876 N.W. 7th Street. Our neighborhood would become the future site of the

Orange Bowl Stadium operational in 1937. It was here that my brother Marvin Aldrich Moore was born on November 24, 1935. Thelma's third birthday was just two days before his birth. Mama had suffered nightmares through the years after Arad died. It was a blessing that with a new son joining the three daughters, the nightmares ceased. In my afflictions over the years, I would remind myself of my mother's great pain of a dead child, a dying child, and a newborn experienced simultaneously. Remembering helped me to keep from wallowing in self-pity.

The year 1935 brought many challenges to our family with our move to 10th Avenue, Marvin's birth and the deaths of both grandmothers. Each lived in Jacksonville, Florida, about 350 miles from us. Travel was difficult in those days, so we seldom saw them. We children were very young and had no memories of either grandmother, or grandfathers as both had died long before any of us were born. Our maternal grandfather was Robert Brian Aldrich, who died May 9, 1909, just three days after my mother's third birthday. Grandfather James Madison Moore died in December 1925. This was the year my parents married – June 6, 1925, which was Dad's 21st birthday. At the time of this writing, I strive to be a good grandmother affectionately called Nana, and great-grandmother called Gigi, and ultimately great-great grandmother called "Triple G" as I felt such a loss not having grandparents when many childhood friends had them.

Since I had not yet finished first grade, I started the second semester at Citrus Grove Elementary and Junior High School for grades 1 through 9. December of 1935, I was chosen out of my class to attend the Dade County Christmas Party for the poor children where I received a beautiful baby doll. All girls attending the event received dolls that were just alike except for a different color of clothing: pink, blue, or yellow. I chose pink and thought she was the prettiest doll I had ever seen. Dad didn't want to acknowledge I went there as he was too proud to take "charity." All the boys at the party received a baseball, glove, and bat. There was ice cream and clowns to entertain us. I know this kindness of strangers made a great impression on all who were lucky enough to be invited.

In the following years, the Orange Bowl Stadium was under construction. All the children enjoyed playing in and around the construction site and at a public playground nearby. People would call us liars when we told them that we were sisters because we looked so different from one other. Nellie had lush auburn colored hair with large brown eyes. Thelma Adele had wavy dark sable hair and brown eyes too. I felt cheated because I had straight, limp blonde hair and blue eyes. A typical middle child I was compliant and often had feelings of being overlooked. At the Orange Bowl Stadium dedication ceremony, Sonja Henie, Olympic Gold Medalist from Norway, along with her troupe of athletes put on an ice show for us. Children in the city were allowed to attend free of charge. I was enthralled! From then on, I decided I wanted to ice skate. What a difficult dream to bring about in the warm climate of Miami with no ice or snow. I would be in my thirties before I lived where that could happen.

# NEW LIFE NEW LESSONS

## 1940 – 1949

Easter Sunday, April 13, 1941, at age 12, I was born again to a living hope in Jesus Christ. I was baptized that evening at Calvary Baptist Church in Miami, Florida, by Pastor Dr. Albert E. Gammage who had led me to the Lord earlier that afternoon sitting on the steps leading up to the front door of the church.

On December 7, 1941, I was swinging in a swing in our carport when the neighbor girl Nevella Lowery came running into our yard yelling, "We're at war!" She was about seven years old at the time and informed us that the Japanese had bombed Pearl Harbor. Nevella's dad was a radio newscaster, so she listened to her dad whenever he was broadcasting the news. At the time I had no idea where Pearl Harbor was but thirty-one years after the attack, I visited Honolulu, Hawaii and toured the memorial in the harbor.

Miami being a coastal city was under a "black out" ban to reduce the loom over the city because German U-boats patrolled the eastern seaboard of America. The nights were darkened as streetlights were painted black on the top half as well as car headlights. No neon lights in the city or lighted billboards, or any other lighting that could be turned off. In the forties there was a movie produced "Moon Over

Miami" with Betty Grable. It was nice to have moon lit nights with such blackout restrictions.

During World War II there was rationing of gas, sugar and meat. My ration card listed that I was 5 feet 1 inch tall when the card was issued. All people needed a ration card for purchasing food for the family. Children had no ration for gasoline.

At school we would have Patriotic Assemblies where we would sing all the songs representing the U.S. Army, U.S. Navy, U.S. Marines, U.S. Army Air Force and the U.S. Coastguard. We had air raid drills and movies showing us what to do if we were bombed with incendiary bombs. Military convoys would drive past our house, and we would wave at the servicemen.

*Turn your eyes upon Jesus,*
*Look full in His wonderful face,*
*And the things of earth will grow strangely dim,*
*In the light of His glory and grace.*

In 1942 Julian Bridges visited our church one Sunday morning and told Mrs. Peck, our department leader, that he came because he wanted to be like Al Gammage, the pastor's son. I was standing nearby and learned one of the most valuable lessons of a lifetime. Mrs. Peck told him, "Julian, Al is as fine a boy as I have ever known, but he is a human being. Someday he may disappoint you or let you down, but if you keep your eyes on Jesus, you will never be disappointed or let down." Al Gammage became a missionary to South Korea serving there 20 years where he was the President of the Korea Baptist Theological Seminary for 12 of those years in Korea. During his 16 plus years in the Philippines Al was Academic Dean of the Asia Baptist Theological Seminary. Julian served as a missionary to Mexico.

Since hearing Mrs. Peck's comment to Julian, nothing in all my life has ever come between me and my Lord other than my own sins even though I have witnessed many things over the years that could have turned me away from the church. But then, people are not GOD. Later in life, a great movie, "For Pete's Sake," produced in the early 1960s, reinforced that as a young black man was told by a member of the motorcycle group that he was witnessing to about the Lord, that no white church in Denver would allow him to worship in their church. His answer, "That's true, but that only tells me something about the people in that congregation, nothing about God."

*Nearness to God is what truly feed my soul.*

Mama's stepfather died in August of 1943. That October while checking on the flat tire of her car Edith Gammage our pastor's wife was hit by a passing car and killed. She was on her way home from choir practice. What I remember most about her was the banner she placed above the chalkboard she used while teaching Scripture in the Ladies' Sunday School class, "Exalt the Christ Who exalted womanhood." This particularly struck a chord with me as our generation in church and society was strongly encouraged to get married, have babies, and know our place in this world.

My brother Robert Owen Moore was born on April 28, 1944. I was a freshman at Miami Senior High School and had just celebrated my 15th birthday on April 4th. Bobby was a beautiful baby with blond curls and a face like Shirley Temple, except his eyes are blue like mine and our dad's while Shirley's are brown. That made it even, my parents now had had three boys and three girls, but Arad was already with the Lord. Bobby is still a joy to me.

Those blond curls, which I didn't have, but thought them prettier than the straight, limp hair on my head. My teens began my life-long pursuit of curls with perms and pin curls.

D-Day invasion on the beaches of Normandy, France, June 6, 1944, was my dad's 40th birthday. Also in June, Nellie graduated from Miami Senior High School at age 16. After graduating Nellie went to work at Western Union where she worked for 42 consecutive years. It was known in Atlanta when Nellie Moore was on the telegraph line. She was so fast that she could take smoke breaks for the tape to catch up with her. During World War II Western Union run mostly by women as the men were in battles both in Europe and the South Pacific. Although some men engineers kept the receivers and transmitters operating. The U.S. Government used Western Union to send notices of military deaths, wounded in action and missing in action as few homes had telephones. We didn't have a phone.

May 1945 brought the war to a close in Europe. In August the Japanese surrendered after two atomic bombs were dropped on Japan: Hiroshima and Nagasaki. On December 23rd I was hit by a car while riding Nellie's bicycle. A young girl was riding on the handlebars. She was tossed into the tall grass beside the road, and I hit the pavement. The rear wheel was twisted metal. It happened right across the street from our home. Gawking strangers filled our house as the firemen painted my scraped skin with iodine. An ambulance arrived and took me to Jackson Memorial Hospital for observation. There I received my first tetanus shot. After a few hours they decided I had only suffered abrasions, nothing worse and released me to go home with my mother. How quickly plans change from going to the Christmas pageant at church to hospital visit instead.

On New Year's Eve 1945, my friend Peggy Roberts and I went downtown to watch the annual Orange Bowl Parade. This was the first Orange Bowl Parade since World War II started. Many military personnel were still in the city as the government didn't want to discharge them all at the same time back into the American workforce. Everyone was in a great mood with the war over. After the parade ended the crowds went wild. Servicemen were circling girls, kissing them, picking them up and carrying them away when trying to catch buses to leave the area. The fire department sprayed the crowd to calm them down. Eventually it was our turn to be harassed as a group of servicemen kept picking Peggy and me up every time, we would try to board a bus to leave for the Watch Night service being held at our church. Finally, two of them said that they would allow us to catch the next bus if we would let them go to church with us. It was okay as both of our parents and families would be at the church, and we would be going home with them as the service ended after the arrival of the New Year – 1946. At the Watch Night service, we had food and fellowship, before midnight all knelt and prayed the old year out and the new year in. The servicemen went to church with us and found their way back to their bases after it was over and we left with our families. No harm, no foul.

A few months later, at Youth for Christ rally at Central Baptist Church in downtown Miami one of those two servicemen who had gone with Peggy and me to our church's Watch Night service came to the rally. He spotted me and came to apologize for his conduct that night, and then thanked me for being the first steppingstone in his life to finding Christ as his savior. He said that New Year's Eve he heard real prayer for the first time and thereafter sought to find God. He had dedicated his life to serving the Lord full time. I had done nothing other than to tell him he could go with us, but thankful God spoke to him through prayer.

January 1946, I started my senior year in high school. By June I only needed three more credits to graduate so I went to summer school and graduated on August 9, 1946, at age 17. In September my dad took me to the Florida National Bank and Trust Company in the Alfred I. DuPont Building in downtown Miami, just as dad encouraged Nellie to go to work at Western Union, and I landed my first post high school job. I first worked in the Proof department and then in the Transit department and became head of the Proof department at age 21. Never was a teller. Mom and Dad knew Nellie excelled in English and I in math. I think in numbers as I have a brain for numbers.

On the eve of my 18th birthday April 3, 1947, my friend Bertha arrived at our home to my dad's explanation of no overnight company that night as our family was expecting the arrival of relatives from Jacksonville. From time-to-time Bertha would stay at our home and other times I would stay at her home. Bertha said she came to ask if I could spend the night at her home. That was good news and permission granted. Bertha and I walked back to her house. Upon our arrival a carload of their relatives had arrived from Ohio and there was no room in either home for Bertha or me. We spent the night sleeping in the car in their yard. The next morning, Bertha and I left for work. At work my throat began to hurt. Co-workers insisted that I go see a doctor in our building. I did and was diagnosed by the doctor with strep throat. After a penicillin shot, I was sent home. That was an unwelcome birthday gift!

I had my first paid vacation in May 1947. Mom, Bertha Ellery and I went to Charleston, South Carolina to visit mom's brother Robby Aldrich who established the first radio station in Charleston. From there we headed north to Baltimore, Maryland and on to Philadelphia, Pennsylvania where we visited Independence Hall. Bertha was thrilled to see silver tableware in the museum with the name Ellery engraved on it. One of her ancestors was a signer of the Constitution of the United States of America.

*Life is full of tests and trials – get ready.*

In 1948 I nearly drowned at Miami Beach when my friend Mary Powell wanted us to swim out to a sandbar. Once she realized she could no longer touch the bottom she was unable to swim. In her panic she pulled me under. Had not Ted Gibson heard her screams and rescued us there never would have been a Linda, Kimberly or Kaitlyn Gibson. (My daughter Linda married John Owen Gibson in 1979.) Ted had been a World War II flying ace in the Pacific theater of war. Earlier in 1948 he was enlisted by the new nation of Israel to head up that nation's air force to fight against five nations who were determined to push all the Israelis into the Mediterranean Sea. God fought for Israel as He had the other five nations fight between themselves as to who was going to have the honor of destroying Israel. In the meantime, the Israelis plucked the enemy off one nation at a time. December 3, 1951, was Ted's funeral in Miami, Florida. He had died in a plane crash in Zurich, Switzerland.

One Sunday afternoon I was driving my dad's pickup truck to the county prison where we were to conduct worship services for the inmates. Three of us were in the cab and eight were in the bed of the truck. I noticed a car coming towards us on the highway careening all over the road. I moved off the highway to the right shoulder to give him space. However, when he was opposite us, he slammed on his brakes to keep from hitting a car and when he did, the brakes locked, and the vehicle skidded across the highway into the side of the truck. I gripped the steering wheel so hard it bowed down on both sides. The people in the back were thrown out. My legs were too weak to stand until I heard that all were alive. Two men were hospitalized, one with broken ribs and the other with a crushed arm. It was touch and go for two months for Freddy with the crushed arm as to whether he would lose it. Thankfully, it was never amputated. That day I never saw the man who hit us as he fled the scene. Two months later I met him in court. He had no driver's license, no vehicle insurance and was driving a borrowed vehicle. The judge fined him $50 and 30 days in jail. My dad had to absorb the $300 damage to his truck. The police officer assured my dad that I had done all I could to avoid the accident by trying to get out of the way.

Dr. Albert E. Gammage, my now deceased pastor, was the one who had started the prison ministry. He would go every Sunday afternoon and preach outside the prison walls to the prisoners looking out the windows no matter what the weather. After the prison authorities allowed worship service inside the prison other churches in the city started going one Sunday a month. By the time I became involved in the prison ministry our church was supplying a worship team once a month. The prisoners always had a spiritual song to sing for us. I enjoyed the good singing.

April 4, 1949, I left my teen years behind and entered my twenties. I was excited as I wanted to be 21 for two reasons: no longer under the legal authority of my parents. (However, my dad informed me that if I lived under his roof, he would be my authority.) and I wanted to be old enough to vote. My dad was absolute authority in our home, large and in-charge. One of my vivid memories of his rule came on a hot summer day in Miami doing the family's ironing. I donned my bathing suit and began to iron on the back porch where there was some air movement only to be told by my father to go and change immediately. He was truly the master of our home.

# NEW FAMILY

## 1950 – 1959

In 1950 I had my 21st birthday and would be able to vote for "Ike" (Dwight D. Eisenhower) in November 1952. I have continued to be a regular voter in all elections even when I lived out of the country.

December 13, 1951, my last name was changed when Rex and I married in Corpus Christi, Texas. He asked me to move to Corpus Christi with him. We eloped and were married in the courthouse. I have been a Cox for over 71 years – a lot longer than the 22 years as a Moore. Rex and I had met when I was 17 and he was 30. My mom would say, "you're not going to marry that old devil, are you?" It became a standard tease between the two of them. However, we were not serious until he returned from fighting for Israel with his good friend Ted Gibson, the same Ted that saved me and my friend from drowning. Rex spoke of sitting alone in a Paris hotel after seeing a lot of the world, wishing he had someone to share life with and thought, "I'll go back and marry Lila." Married at the ages of 22 and 35 didn't sound as far apart as 17 and 30.

In January 1952 I applied for employment at two banks in Corpus Christi, Texas. I interviewed at both banks on the same day. Corpus Christi National Bank offered me $165 per month salary (no overtime) to sort checks for the bookkeepers. I explained to them I had an interview with First State Bank later that day and would call them after my other appointment. I was told that I did not want to work at First State Bank as they worked long hours every day into the night.

At First State Bank Mr. McKenzie the Executive Vice-President offered me the position of Head of the Proof Department at $165 per month with no overtime. He leveled with me and said the proof department worked long hours every day, but he was hoping I could find out why and correct the problem since I had experience. That was a challenge. I like challenges and accepted the job offer that Friday. I was to report to work the following Monday morning. I called the other bank to tell them that I had accepted the position at First State Bank and was told that I would be sorry.

On Monday when I showed up for work at First State Bank, Mr. McKenzie took me to the Proof Department and introduced me to the other employees as the new Head of the Proof Department. About two hours later he called me out of the room and asked what I thought about their system. I informed him that I knew nothing about their system, but I knew why they were working such long hours. He rocked back on his heels as I told him what I had been doing those two hours. I was checking one operator's work. Her errors were so numerous that the only thing to do was keep correcting them. That much inaccuracy would keep workers a long time after hours trying to balance each day. He asked if he should fire the lady. I told him not to fire her if she could work in the bookkeeping department sorting checks for the bookkeepers to post and not enter data herself (like the job I was offered at the Corpus Christi National Bank). He removed her immediately from the IMB sorting machine and moved her into the Bookkeeping Department. We balanced and finished at 4 p.m. my first day on the job. They had been working until 9 or 10 p.m. nightly with no overtime compensation.

After six months there, Rex wanted me to apply for work at the Naval Air Station (NAS) and work in Civil Service. I would have a five-day work week same as him. The bank was open six days a week and Saturday was our busiest day. During my six months at the bank, we never had to work late. At Rex's insistence, I applied at the NAS and offered a job which paid twice what I was making at the bank. I gave two weeks' notice to the bank that I would be leaving to work at the Naval Air Station. My last day at the bank my co-workers took me out to lunch. One of them sheepishly told me that before they had ever seen me, they decided that they would not cooperate with me as they thought Betty should have been made Head of the Proof Department and not an outsider. I told them I thought we had gotten along very well from the beginning. Then they all said that they were so happy to get off work at 4 p.m. rather than 9 or 10 p.m. they were glad I had come.

I started work at the Naval Air Station in Corpus Christi in June 1952. In January 1953 we had a three-day weekend. I traveled with my friends Joe and Mary Speed to Waco, Texas where they left me with friends that I had known in Miami. They continued north to go see Mary's parents and would pick me up on Monday on their way back to Corpus Christi.

*Trust is what God grows in our hearts*
*when we give our doubts over to*
*the love of God. – Mike Donehey*

My first night at the Smith's home they told me that when the lights went out the rats came out! They didn't have a guest bedroom as they had three young daughters using the other bedroom. A bed was made for me to sleep on the couch in the living room in front of the fireplace. Truly when the lights went out in no time, I could hear the rats moving around me. I was afraid that they would soon be running all over me. I prayed that the Lord would send them away, but while I was praying, I kept expecting to feel them running on me. I recalled a Bible verse which states, "As your faith is, so shall it be." I was at the point where I had to believe God's Word or make a fool of myself because I was approaching hysteria. God gave me the faith to believe. I prayed and believed that He would remove the rats and HE DID! I went peacefully to sleep trusting the One with whom all things are possible. My second night there, the rats didn't even bother to come out. I learned a powerful truth that night. God is true to His word.

Since Rex was now 36 years old, we did not want to wait long to have a family. Because I was not pregnant, we both saw doctors trying to figure out why. My doctor painted me with some medication internally and then gave us a temperature chart to keep determining if I was ovulating. After 40 days of chart keeping, Rex went by to see my doctor and showed him the chart. One look at the temperature chart and Dr. Lingenfelder said that I was as pregnant as I would ever be, and due on November 1st. Since Rex could not call me at work, he proceeded to broadcast the news all around Corpus Christi to everyone he saw that day in town. When I arrived home from work, he was there to meet me. No sooner had Rex told me the news than the phone rang. When I answered, my friend Mary told me how hurt she was that Nelda knew that I was pregnant before she knew. I told Mary that if she had known the news for five minutes that she would have known it longer than I had. Since she knew before I did – she forgave me for not telling her first.

On November 1, 1954, at 1:07 p.m. there was Pamela Sue. Since I had a spinal block for delivery, I watched the doctor tie and cut the umbilical cord. What a marvel to behold, I was speechless as two co-workers had told me that I was carrying a boy. Both said they had never been wrong, but this time they were. I was not disappointed – just surprised.

I worked until late September before her birth but did not return to the work force again until both girls had gone to college. That was our agreement before children were born to us that I would not work outside the home and leave our children for someone else to nurture and raise. I have never regretted that decision. Our children were far more important to us than things. Thankful that God made that possible as not all mothers have that option.

I loved being Pamela Sue's mom and we called her Susie from day one. Susie was named after my Aunt Sue, Mattie Sue Evans. She was such a happy delightful baby and so smart. She laughed out loud the day after she was born. Sitting up the day she was 5 months old. Pulled herself up and stood the day she was 5 months and 12 days old. Walked unassisted for the first time when she was 7 months old. By 8 ½ months she was walking all the time and soon running. Started talking at 8 ½ months. And before Linda was born, she would tell us the word that Rex or I had spelled in conversation for her not to know what we were talking about in her presence. But Susie knew.

*For the LORD is good;*
*his steadfast love endures forever, and*
*his faithfulness to all generations.*
*Psalm 100:5*

With Pamela Sue being such a joy to us we wanted a sibling for her. We did not want her to be an only child. Again, back to the temperature chart. When the doctor saw it, he said that the baby was due on October 8th. Sure enough, on October 8, 1956, at 12:18 a.m. (she just barely waited until her due date) Linda Diane made her entrance into the world.

Two weeks before her birth we had traveled the 400 miles from Dallas, where we had moved in May 1956, to Corpus Christi for her birth. Along the way Rex and I discussed names, David Oliver for a boy and Linda Diane for a girl. When we arrived at our home in Corpus Christi (the renters had just vacated at a very convenient time for us) Susie immediately walked throughout the house while Rex and I were still standing in the kitchen. She came back to the kitchen and asked where Linda was. She didn't ask about David.

The day after Linda was born Rex brought Susie to the hospital. In those days children were not allowed into patient rooms. The nurses watched Susie down in the lobby and Rex brought me down in a wheelchair. He placed Susie on my lap. She looked up at me and asked, "Someday you going to tell me all about it?" She would not have her 2nd birthday for another 3 ½ weeks. I merely said, "Someday."

As it turned out, Susie was not too thrilled having a sister since the baby took up a lot of mommy time. Susie had been her mommy's only interest and she wasn't excited about sharing me with Linda. Thankfully they are best friends now.

On Susie's 2nd birthday we drove back to Dallas with our new baby girl. Two weeks later we were on our way to Florida to visit my family and let them see Linda.

Christmas 1956 was spent in St. Louis, Missouri with Rex's family. It was the first time that Dad Cox had ever seen all his children together at one time. It was a wonderful reunion. Rex was 40 and his youngest sister was six. Linda was the youngest one present at age two and one-half months. Before Linda was three months old, she had traveled more than 5,000 miles by car. And she hasn't stopped going yet.

The next trip was to see his mother Lelah Westerfield in Bedford, Indiana (Rex's father and mother divorced when he was a young lad, and both eventually remarried) for her to see her youngest grandchild. During the trip I got sick and then the girls were sick as the illness passed around our family. By the time we returned to Dallas, Texas we were in recovery mode.

April 2, 1957, a killer tornado made a path on the west side of Dallas. We had just moved that morning from Dallas to Irving. The path of the tornado went between where we had lived and the office where Rex worked two miles away. The next morning when I took Linda to the pediatrician we saw across the street from the doctor's office where the tornado had leveled a service station and one of the eleven people that were killed had died there. We chose the right day to leave Dallas.

*Where will my current choices lead me?*

Rex was Executive Director of the Texas Mobile Home Association, the reason we had moved to Dallas. In October 1958 he resigned and went into business selling insurance as he was tired of traveling and being gone from the family. It took many long trips to cover Texas.

Christmas 1957 was spent in Silver Springs, Florida at my parent's home. Marvin and his family were also there with their baby girl Lydia. Linda took off walking the day Lydia was born August 25, 1957. They had a son Jeff who was six months older than Linda and he wanted to trade Lydia for Linda. Jeff and Linda have always been close friends and cousins.

Christmas 1958 when Linda was two years old, she told me that she had something she wanted to tell me. When I asked what, she said, "Santa is coming to town and going to bring Mommy a dolly." She presented the doll we had given her for Christmas and said, "Here's your dolly, HO, HO, HO!" Linda never liked dolls. She was interested in action.

*Am I better today than I was yesterday?*

In February 1959 Rex was asked to go to Louisville, Kentucky for an interview with the Board of Directors of the Indiana Mobile Home Association, which later became the Indiana Manufacturing Housing Association. They were seeking a new director since the current director was stricken with cancer and could not continue. He was hired and we moved to Indianapolis on April 20, 1959, when Susie was four and one-half years old and Linda two and one-half years. Indiana not as large as Texas meant Rex could be home most nights.

I had just celebrated my 30th birthday in Texas before the move to Indiana. We had pulled our small mobile home behind our car from Texas to Indiana and lived in it until we found a house to purchase. After several months of looking, we found a three-bedroom, bath and half bath, open living room, dining area and kitchen with an attached one car garage. It was in a nice neighborhood with many trees on a large lot.

It was a good choice because a new elementary school Chapelwood Elementary was built, and Linda entered first grade there the year it opened. Susie went on a bus to Westgate Elementary School for her first and second grades but entered her third grade at Chapelwood.

It was a blessing. Later a new junior high and high school were built on Girls School Road. From kindergarten through high school our community was well provided with education. 6746 West 16th Street was to be our home for ten blessed years. The only place I ever really missed when moving away.

During our first summer in Indiana Rex had a trip to Elkhart, the heart of the mobile home manufacturing industry, to get acquainted with the people in the Indiana Mobile Home Association that he had come to lead. The headquarters are in Indianapolis, the State Capitol, for legislative and lobbying purposes.

While Rex was gone, I decided it was a good time for a total fast and prayer (no food or drink) for three days and nights. The girls were young enough not to notice their mom not eating or drinking and I could prepare their meals for them. I wanted a fresh encounter with my Lord and surrendered my life completely to Him.

Life became a great adventure as my Lord began to reveal Himself to me in many ways. My life became a continual "prayer walk."

Our first Indiana snow was Thanksgiving Day 1959. What a beautiful day it was celebrated with a thankful heart.

Our first Christmas in Indiana was great fun with our two girls, now five and three years old.

# NORTHERN EXPOSURE

## 1960 – 1969

The 1960 winter in Indiana was very cold for us Southerners. We were delighted with the beauty of snow. That first Indiana winter we went ice skating on a nearby frozen lake. It was fun watching Susie and Linda ice skating for the first time at ages five and three. At age 30 I was able to stay upright. However, I did end up with pneumonia during our first winter in Indiana.

December 1960 both daughters and I drove from Indianapolis to Texas to take a friend home. It was wonderful seeing old friends in Corpus Christi. Our friend remained in Corpus Christi and on our way back to Indiana we stopped in Dallas to see more friends. At 4 a.m., the day of departure for Indiana I carried my two sleeping daughters to the station wagon and laid them on the bed made in the back. I drove east for about two hours when my rear tire blew. It was still dark at 6 a.m. I awoke the girls, dressed them and started walking in the dark along the divided highway heading back in the direction from which we had come as I had passed a service station not long before the tire blew. In a moment, a car was pulling up behind us and I prayed it would be a woman. It was, and she drove us to the service station. The station attendant was alone. I told him my situation (flat and no spare tire). He locked his gas pumps and his cash register. Then told me he would try to find a used tire and for me to stay in his station until he returned. The station attendant was gone for about an hour and fortunately no customers came during his absence. Upon his return he closed the gas station and drove us to our vehicle. He had already changed the tire and only charged me $4. It was a good used tire as it lasted as long as we owned the vehicle. God continually watches over me and answers my prayers.

> *Blessed are those who dwell in your house,*
> *ever singing your praise! Selah.*
> *Psalm 84:4*

Susie entered first grade at West Lake Elementary School in 1961 where she would spend her first two years of schooling. The bus ride to and from school was upsetting to her stomach and we realized later she had motion sickness which continues to plague her.

That same year we brought into our home an 18-year-old foster son, Wayne. Our home was markedly different, having a teenage boy in addition to our two young girls. Wayne didn't bathe frequently and if he took off his shoes there was an unbelievably unpleasant odor. The only reason I mention this is because of a funny incident. One day while I was ironing clothes in the kitchen, Wayne came home and walked through the kitchen on his way to his bedroom. A few minutes later Linda entered the kitchen through the back door and asked, "Is brother home?" I told her that he was, and she replied, "I thought so, I smell him." He had merely walked through the room. Soon I heard the shower running. After a while Wayne came into the kitchen where I was still ironing and with a sheepish look on his face said, "I heard what Linda said." He was now bathed and wearing clean clothes.

January 1962 my mother was in Indiana with us. We had been to Florida for Christmas, and she returned home with us. Rex was out of town, and I needed to drive our foster son Wayne to the bus line. The temperature was 12 degrees below zero. About two miles from the house, we ran out of gasoline (the car's fuel gauge did not work). By the time the car rolled to a stop, a man coming towards us in a pickup truck turned around in the road and backed up to our car. He jumped out and chained my car to his truck without speaking a word. He towed us less than a mile to a service station, then jumped out and removed the chain and drove off without ever speaking. He did not seem to be dressed warmly. We were now next to the gas pumps and I with no cash. I walked inside the service station and there was my husband's bookkeeper, Billie Winkler. She loaned me $4 to fill the tank and I repaid it to her that afternoon when I went to pick up Wayne. Rex had left a check at home for me to cash. I have always wondered if I saw my guardian angel that day remembering the Scripture which says, "for thereby some have entertained angels unawares."

The goal of bringing Wayne into our home was him being able to transition from foster care to living on his own. Wayne successfully launched into adulthood a brief time later.

Our country was on edge dealing with Cuban missile crisis in 1962 when President John F. Kennedy was having a showdown with the Soviets. The Cold War was an intense time for Americans.

*In tough times remind yourself of who God truly is
and what He has done for you.*

The year 1963 was full of many events, but the big ones in my world were: September 12th our church burned down, October 31st four of our church members were killed in the Halloween explosion at the Indianapolis Coliseum, and the world knew about November 22nd when President John F. Kennedy was assassinated in Dallas, Texas on my sister's 31st birthday.

The night our church members were killed in the explosion along with almost 70 others plus hundreds of wounded, the hospitals all around Indianapolis were overrun with the multitude of patients. It was a dreadful shock as we had just seen our four friends the night before they died. The newspaper showed multiple pictures of funerals and lined up caskets around our city. It is one of the worst disasters in the history of the state. I lost 10 pounds in 10 days as I couldn't eat. Our family was heading for the coliseum that night to go to the *Holiday on Ice* show and had it not been for our two daughters complaining of a stomachache (too much candy at school) we would have been there ourselves. Our girls were pretending to be sick because they wanted to go "Trick or Treating" in the neighborhood with their friends, but their dad made plans for us to be at the ice show. This is one time I was very thankful our girls changed the plan because "the heart of man plans his way, but the LORD establishes his steps" (Proverbs 16:9).

November 22nd I was in Chicago with two of my neighbors and we were at a service station getting our car filled up when the man pumping our gas said, "They just shot your President." He didn't say, "Our" President. Odd things we remember. It was a dark rainy night in northern Indiana, and we listened on the car radio the four-hour drive back to Indianapolis. That event left everybody numb. And for our church family, we were already traumatized.

January 1964 my sister Adele, as she preferred to be called, and her son Jay arrived right after our 15-inch snowfall, the most in fifty years in Indianapolis. They had an opportunity for a free ride to visit as friends were in Florida and offered to bring them to us. However, Adele said she didn't want to make the trip unless I could guarantee snow as neither of them had ever seen snow. I wrote her a letter and made a rash promise that if we didn't have snow we would drive north until we found some. After posting that letter I realized it was a foolish promise as our girls were in school and I couldn't take them out of school to search for snow. Also, I didn't really have money to go traveling. I began to ask God to send snow so Adele wouldn't hold me to the promise I had made. God answered abundantly. Adele sculpted a beautiful horse head with mane flowing in the snow. We all had a blast with the bounty of snow. When friends heard about my prayers for snow, they pleaded with me not to ever pray for snow again. The city was paralyzed as they weren't equipped to manage the amount of snowfall.

Adele and Jay decided to live in Indianapolis, which they did until the winter of 1970 when they moved to Baton Rouge, Louisiana.

The sixties were the years the neighborhood kids hung out at our house. It was good for me because then I knew what was going on with my children as our yard was the place to play. During those years, the neighborhood practiced zone parenting. Many birthday parties with cake and ice cream were celebrated at the homes up and down our street.

*Decision-Making*
*Easy as Inhaling and Exhaling*

One day I had a station wagon loaded with clothing and other donated items collected from church and asked God to show me which of two missions the goods should be given. "Lord, if You want me to give the goods to Wheeler Mission then provide a parking place in front of their facility. If You want me to take the gear to the Edna Martin Center, then do not provide parking at Wheeler Mission as I pass there on my way to the other Center." When I drove to Wheeler Mission God reserved parking place at the front door. I parked and got out. The Lord even provided the dime for the parking meter. Over the years I have delivered donations for both missions as God directed my steps.

While we were members at Lynhurst Baptist Church the Lay Institute for Evangelism (LIFE) conducted by Campus Crusade for Christ came for six days and nights. I signed up for the morning sessions because the girls were in school, and no childcare was needed. Rex attended the evening sessions while I stayed home with the girls. Every evening, I would wait for Rex to return home and hear his comments. LIFE was not anything like we expected. Both of us thought it would be training in Scripture memorization and how to use it when sharing with others about our Lord. For me it was utterly life changing.

The first session of LIFE the instructor gave this comparison of a Christian's life. If a toy electric train were running around the tracks and a metal bar was placed across the tracks it would short circuit the power and the train would stop. He said the entire electric power of the city of Indianapolis could not move that train with the metal bar short circuiting that power. He said that is what sin does in a Christian's life if not confessed and turned from. Sin short circuits the power of God in your life. Then he had us separate and sit alone somewhere in the auditorium. We were each given a sheet of paper and told to write down any sins we needed to confess. The instructor told us to be honest as God already knew. No one would look at another's paper as we would take it home with us and destroy it when finished. About ten minutes later he told us to write on our paper First John 1:9, "If we confess our sins, He is faithful and just to forgive us our sins and to cleanse us from all unrighteousness." I wrote it down on my paper, but what the instructor said next socked me between the eyes: "It is not enough to write it down because if you do not believe that God has forgiven you of your confessed sins, which is the SIN of UNBELIEF." He explained we are only variable, "if we." No "if" on God's part. Up until then I had felt defeated in my Christian walk, but now this very heavy burden lifted because I chose to believe God.

The second session of LIFE was spiritual breathing. Exhaling was confession and inhaling was asking the Holy Spirit to fill us. No need to make a list as we had the day before. The instructor shared with us if we were filled with God's Holy Spirit, the Spirit of God would convict us when we sinned. We only needed to confess any sin as soon as we were convicted (exhale) and appropriate the filling of His Spirit (inhale). Waiting until bedtime prayers to confess rather than immediately upon conviction by the Holy Spirit made you an easy target for the enemy of your soul.

By the end of the week, we were out visiting people in the community taking a survey and sharing our faith with those who were interested. Several made decisions to become Christ followers.

*God uses His Word to change hearts.*
*— Franklin Graham*

On Sunday afternoon, we went south to where Rex's mom lived in Bryantsville, Indiana. He shared with his mom, and she received

Christ into her life at age 75. Rex had talked with her on other occasions, and she was not interested, but this time she was. Rex said he knew it was because he confessed his sins and got right with God, then God's power did the rest. Rex had quit tithing while we were living in Texas because the pastor was embezzling from the church. He learned that he was sinning and excused his sin when he was not tithing to the Lord because of someone else's sin.

I began a weekly Women's Bible Study in my home using Campus Crusade for Christ study materials. It was a study guide where each person searched the Scriptures on their own and wrote in the booklet what they discovered. Each week we shared among our group what our Lord had revealed to us. There were seven different denominations represented among the 22 regular attendees. The interesting thing was that the only differing understanding of Scripture was regarding baptism and the eternal security of the believer. All other doctrines of all seven denominations came to the same conclusion of what Scripture taught. There is great unity when the Bible is the plumbline and not the teachings of man or religious traditions.

At about this same time I started hosting a weekly Good News Club using materials from Child Evangelism Fellowship for children. There were 45 regular attenders, wall to wall children in our home, all elementary school aged kids. I taught using flannel graph pictures to illustrate the Bible stories. During those years 21 children made professions of faith in Christ and went on to serve God.

*Weeping may tarry for the night,*
*but joy comes with the morning.*
*Psalm 30:5b*

On April 28, 1969, my brother Bob's 25th birthday, our mother was diagnosed with cancer. I had just turned 40 on the 4th. He didn't get a good birthday gift that day, nor did the rest of us. The exploratory surgery took place in Ocala, Florida and my family lived 925 miles away in Indianapolis. As soon as school was out for the summer, my sister Adele with her son Jay, both daughters, Rex and I drove to Florida. My older sister Nellie had taken leave from work to care for Mom until I could get there and relieve Nellie to return to work. However, it wasn't working out for our mom with eleven grandkids running in and out of her room. My dad was about to go broke trying to feed a total of 16 people three meals a day. Rex and Adele needed to return to work. A man who had been a family friend for decades was also staying at the Craft Motel that my parents were buying. Without all the particulars, we took the family friend to live with his family. My brother Bob took his family of five home to Miami. Two of brother Marvin's five children went to Miami to stay with their maternal grandmother. I took my two, Marvin's two daughters and my nephew Jay back to Indianapolis. Only one grandchild Jeffery remained behind to run the motel's front desk while Dad and Marvin were doing construction on the RV Park behind the motel. Georgia, Marvin's wife, took care of mom in peace and quiet.

Five weeks later, on Friday evening July 25th, my family called from Florida to tell me that Mom had been taken to the hospital and it was time for us all to gather. Mom didn't give up on life until the first astronauts to the moon had returned safely to earth as she kept praying that God would bring them safely back to earth. And God did. Right after they were rescued from the sea and aboard ship, she gave up her struggle to live.

It was a frantic evening as Rex was out of town and I couldn't locate my sister by phone. (Remembering this was before cellphones.) The car I would drive to Florida was at the airport where Rex had left it parked while he was in Evansville, Indiana. It was 11 p.m. before Rex returned my phone call. He said he would be home in the morning and then we could start the drive to Florida. I finally reached my sister only to hear her say she had to work until noon. We eventually left Indianapolis in the early afternoon. That evening around 6:30 p.m. in Tennessee, Rex wanted us to stay overnight at a motel and continue traveling the next morning. I told him if he insisted that we stay overnight he needed to get something from the drug store to make me sleep as I couldn't sleep knowing my mother was on her deathbed. He finally agreed we would drive as long as we could. We had two cars, three adults and five children. I spent the entire night either relieving Rex or Adele from driving. We reached Ocala at 6:30 a.m. Sunday morning July 27th only to find out that my mother had died at 6:30 p.m. the night before while we were on our way. It was my most difficult moment.

Tuesday, July 29th, Mom's funeral was held at First Baptist Church in Ocala, Florida with all siblings and our families present. That was the day I had planned to return to Coney Island in Cincinnati with a friend and her two children. We had such a wonderful time at Coney Island earlier in the summer we decided we would go again. Plans often change.

After the funeral we left for Miami where May Love Moore was to be interned. At the cemetery, our Miami friends came to offer condolences. We stayed overnight and then headed back to Ocala, 300 miles north.

*Surrender to God is the path to freedom.*

In September we moved out of the home where we had lived for 10 wonderful years and rented a mobile home until our new home was ready for occupancy. Our new home was situated on seven acres of land to accommodate both of our daughters' horses.

We were buying a double-wide (24 feet x 58 feet) mobile home. The home was delivered to the land and a foundation had to be prepared before setup. Soon after the two halves were on the property thieves came and stole our new washer and dryer plus all the boxed drapery. Our furniture was safe in storage. The deputy sheriff came, interviewed us and saw the note I had written taped to the double-wide refrigerator "Dear Thieves, what you need is forgiveness from God rather than this refrigerator or stove." I put tracts inside the frig and the stove figuring if the thieves returned and took those two appliances, they would take the Word of God with them. Whether the thieves returned to steal the other appliances or not, I'll never know, but they were not stolen. Fortunately, I was able to forgive the thieves and the loss.

We moved into our home on Bridge Port Road in early November and at Thanksgiving, Marvin and his family visited us for the first time in Indiana with their five children. Their daughter Lydia stayed with us for the remainder of that school year.

*Don't Stop Praying,*

Life can become interesting with three teenage girls in one house.

*"While the earth remains, seedtime and harvest, and cold and heat, and summer and winter, and day and night shall not cease."*

*Genesis 8:22*

# DECEIVED, BUT NOT FOR LONG

## 1970 – 1979

1970 offered us a bitter winter in Indianapolis. We were in our new home, but it was not fully prepared for winter. The water froze and another load of sand was dumped over the water well area to keep the well from freezing. The arctic air blew under our house as we did not have "skirting" around our double-wide mobile home to help insult from the elements. We had huge electric bills and difficulty keeping warm.

This is when Adele with her son Jay left Indianapolis to move south to Baton Rouge, Louisiana. She drove a truck with her household furniture and gear right out of the snow. She made it safely to Baton Rouge and resided there for some years.

*Obedience doesn't always guarantee everything will go our way or even what we perceive to be God's way.*

In April 1971 during Spring Break from school, the three girls and I headed south to Florida with my prayer partner traveling with us. After visiting with my widowed dad and brother Marvin and his family at Silver Springs, we went further south to Hollywood, Florida to visit my brother Bob and his family. While there with Bob, he wanted us to go to "The House" in Ft. Lauderdale, where Teen Challenge ministered to runaway teens. We arrived during their prayer meeting. Immediately I felt ill at ease as the participants looked as though they were in trances praying in "tongues." Had I arrived alone, I would have exited right away. After that ended and many present began to give testimonies of "miracles" they had witnessed or had happened to themselves. Later in the meeting a former Southern Baptist gave his testimony which was the most convincing of anything I had heard or seen thus far. At the close of his talk, he invited those wishing to receive the baptism of the Holy Spirit to come forward. My brother Bob and nephew Jeff went forward. The speaker Norvell Hayes prayed over Bob, but nothing "happened" and Norvell told my brother to keep seeking it and eventually it would happen to him. It never did. In the meantime, a group had surrounded Jeff and were laboring over him in "prayer" and massaging his throat and trying to coax the "tongues" out of him. It was April 7, 1971, Jeff's 15th birthday. Eventually they gave up and Jeff never experienced "it." The speaker talked with my prayer partner and me asking us where we were from. After telling him we were from Indianapolis he informed us that he and the others in the room would be at the Marriott Hotel in our city in May. He invited us to attend.

I had read two remarkably interesting books, "The Challenging Counterfeit" and "Dealing with the Devil." After reading both books I was convinced that the devil would not deceive me. Very soon thereafter I was deceived – thankfully, not for long.

In May, we attended those meetings at the Marriott Hotel with Rex joining us. The first night an invitation was given to any who had any physical condition needing healing. I went forward to the front of the room for healing of my breast in which I had recently discovered a lump. Norvell Hayes prayed over me and commanded in the Name of Jesus for the lump to come out. Afterwards he told me to thank God every day for His healing and the lump would go away.

In the meantime, all three of our teenage girls, went forward for the baptism of the Holy Spirit. I was unaware because of the crowd. Driving home all three girls were mumbling in "tongues," but all three sounded different from each other. We took my prayer partner home and then we arrived home with the girls continuing to speak in "tongues". It was a school night, so the girls went to bed.

To shorten this episode in our lives, fast forward to Saturday night, the final night of the rally. All six of us attended the final night. Again, the invitation was for those needing healing. Rex went forward hoping for healing of his blind right eye. My prayer partner went forward for healing of her deaf ear.

Sunday morning, we were back at Bethesda Baptist Church as usual. That evening, we returned to church and after the service an usher approached me and said that Pastor Tyler wanted to see me in his office. Since the girls had gone to church an hour earlier for the Youth meeting, they left for home. Gathered in the Pastor's office was Pastor Tyler, some of the deacons and the Youth Pastor. The Pastor informed me he had heard about us going to the Rally and asked how I got mixed up in it. I explained to the group about being in Florida and my brother Bob asking us to go with him to the "House" operated by Teen Challenge.

The Pastor and others in the room told me various things they had known and observed regarding this teaching. Pastor Tyler said that if I believed what was being "taught" by this group that I could not continue to teach six grade girls on Sunday mornings at our church. However, he said next Sunday is a week away and gave me a book to read from his library written by Dr. Gramacke of Cedarville College in Ohio. He knew that I loved and taught God's Word. He prayed John 7:17 "If any man is willing to do His will, he shall know of the teaching, whether it is of God, or whether I speak from myself." He asked me to read the book and then tell him what I believed. He said if I agreed with the interpretations of scripture in the book, then there was no reason to quit teaching in the church. If I disagreed, then I could no longer teach there. He didn't want division in the church.

Arriving home with book in hand, I was greeted by our three girls. They were waiting for me to tell them what the Pastor talked with me about. I shared what Pastor Tyler had said and the book I was to read. They said he doesn't understand because he hasn't experienced it. Since it was late, and they had to get up early for school, I suggested we all go to bed. We would discuss this after I had read the book while they were in school. I headed down the hall to prepare for bed. When I came out of the bathroom my niece Lydia said, "Aunt Lila, if you would let the three of us pray over you then you would experience the baptism of the Holy Spirit and then you would know as we do." I reiterated that I would spend tomorrow searching the Scriptures for the truth. They insisted upon praying over me. I knew they could not harm me in any way because I would be praying to God myself and not opening my spirit to just anything "out there."

We went to the living room, and I was going to sit in a chair so they could pray over me. Lydia said, "Aunt Lila, you have to stand up because it feels so great when you fall down." I stood and prayed silently while they all three prayed over me in "tongues." Sue began to cry so I asked them to stop, and I said, "Sue, I am going to heaven when I die, with or without tongues, because my destiny is not determined by tongues." Let's go to bed and talk about this after school tomorrow.

*The truth of God does not shift with changing emotions.*

Since I couldn't get to sleep, Isaiah 26:3 came into my mind, "Thou will keep him in perfect peace whose mind is stayed upon Thee." I kept my mind focused on Jesus and went peacefully to sleep.

After the girls left for school and Rex had not left for work, I told him about the Pastor's talk with me with the deacons and Youth Pastor present. I also told him that Pastor Tyler loaned me a book to guide me to Scripture references to search out for myself. Rex remained home as long as he could and together, we examined the book. After he left, I called my prayer partner and told her what had happened. I gave her Scripture references listed in the book and we agreed that we would both spend the morning studying and then talk again at noon.

At noon when we compared our study notes we both agreed that "tongues" was not something we should seek. When the girls arrived home from school they came rushing in and asked what the answer was. I told them that "tongues" was not something to "practice" or seek. Lydia was disappointed, Sue was perplexed, and Linda soon came back and told me that she was going to test the "spirit" and find out if it was from God or not. I asked her how she planned to "test the spirit." She said that she was going to pray and ask God to forgive her if she was wrong, and to take the "tongues" away from her if they were not from Him. That was a real test because ever since she started speaking in "tongues" the previous Wednesday evening the "tongues" would spill out of her month every time she prayed or read God's Word without any effort on her part to do so. I then asked Sue and Lydia to test the spirit of "tongues" with Linda and me. After we four finished praying "tongues" left our house and did not return.

*God is in the whisper – you must be close to hear the whisper.*

During the time they were under the influence of the "tongues," Linda's mind was in confusion. A straight "A" student she failed her first school test ever. She had difficulty with her studies as the "tongues" took over her mind. As soon as she was released from the "tongues" her mind was sharp again.

I notified Pastor Tyler of our findings. He asked me to give my testimony at a prayer meeting that Wednesday evening. At the meeting Pastor asked anyone who had a testimony to share to stand and speak (after being acknowledged to speak as there were around 400 people present). Several in the congregation had something to share so after I stood, he asked me to come to the front and speak. I was a bit nervous about speaking, but people were praying for me. A complete calm came over me as I shared it with the church. Through this the Lord taught me the truth of Proverbs 3:5 and 6, "Trust in the Lord with all your heart, and do not lean on your own understanding. In all your ways acknowledge Him, and He will make your paths straight." I realized how foolish it had been for me to think that the devil would never deceive me again after reading those other two books – and he deceived me immediately because my trust was in what I thought I knew rather than trusting in the Lord Who knows all things.

*Don't worry about how much faith you have.*
*Focus on what or who you put it in. – Tony Evans*

After I had spoken at church and returned to where I had been sitting, a lady in front of me turned around and said that she knew that I went through the fire for her and wanted to talk with me after the service.

This lady said that she and her husband had moved to California to be with his family who were Pentecostals. They were going to the church with them. During one of the services, she was flat on her back in a trance when the Lord told her to get up. She did and said to the people they were all a bunch of hypocrites, and she was not coming back. The couple left California and returned to Indiana. I asked her how she came to our church. A friend had brought them, but she had been troubled about whether she had been right when she spoke out in the church in California rebuking them. God comforted her with my testimony as she knew then she was in the right place. And leaving California had been the right move for them.

Some insights from those meetings: never was there any invitation given to receive salvation in Jesus Christ – only to receive physical healing. I don't remember Jesus being mentioned. Jesus said in John 16:13 and 14, "But when He, the Spirit of truth, comes, He will guide you into all truth; for He will not speak of His own initiative, but whatever He hears, He will speak; and He will disclose to you what is to come. He shall glorify Me; for He shall take of what is Mine, and shall disclose it to you." We who went forward for healing were not healed, nor did we fall backwards to the floor like others. They had no power over us for harm or for good.

*Seek the Giver of blessings not just the blessings.*

Later through prayer the lump in my breast was gone, but not before the "tongues" were gone from our home.

During this decade I began taking Moody Bible Institute studies completing seven courses. It was very enriching. Studying God's Word always produces a yield of good fruit.

At this same time, I was leading a Bible study on Wednesday mornings. One Wednesday I just didn't have any strength to go. I knelt beside my bed and asked God to give me His strength as I was too exhausted to go. Physically I could feel His strength pour into my body. I arose from my knees fully renewed in strength and went to lead the study. He can meet any need we have.

Always in a rush to get to church, which was a good 30-minute drive, my brother Bob visiting and traveling with us to Bethesda Baptist Church one evening. Bob was reading while I drove. I hit the railroad tracks and became a little airborne. Never looking up Bob said, "Hello, God." Then he explained to me that my driving was to the glory of God.

One summer Rex took our only phone out of the house for three months because a friend called me daily and would keep me on the phone for hours. The conversations were a continuous dialogue of her woes. My head cocked endlessly to one side or the other cradling the receiver to my ear had caused extreme pain in my neck. Even though we had an extra-long phone cord with which I could reach the kitchen and laundry room I was constantly tied to the phone in the hallway, taking me away from other activities and chores. This was Rex's solution to break the cycle of these long and unfruitful conversations and help alleviate the pain in my neck.

*Rock bottom is the foundation of God.*

Sue attended night school for her last credit for graduation from high school as she was already employed as a secretary at IMHA (Indiana Manufactured Housing Association) with her dad. Late afternoon after I returned from grocery shopping, Linda said she would go feed the horses. She soon came inside screaming, "Gypsy is dying!" When I asked her what was wrong, she said that her insides were coming out. She grabbed the phone book and tried to find the phone number for the vet. I stepped outside, looked around the garage into the pasture, and there was Gypsy lying on her side heaving. As I continued to watch Gypsy a foal's head appeared. I ran into the house and shouted to Linda that Gypsy was giving birth. The foal was looking around like it wanted out while still half inside the mother. Linda knelt and gently pulled the foal from the mother.

Linda asked what to do next. I explained to her I would get a knife and new white shoelaces to tie the cord in two places and she could cut the cord between the ties (I had watched the doctor do this when I delivered Sue). With those supplies, Linda did the job. Then she pulled the placenta out. The filly was like limp cooked spaghetti, but not for long. In less than an hour she was up and kicking, frolicking about.

Linda called the boarded mare's owner Darla who had no idea that Gypsy was pregnant. A shocking surprise for us all. Darla and her mother came to see their prize.

Our church was having revival meetings that week, so Linda and I went inside and got ready for church. Gypsy and her filly were doing fine so we left.

When Sue returned home from school, she knew nothing about the filly. It was now after dark, and she was home alone. There was a knock on the back door. Sue looked out and saw a woman, she did not recognize who said, "We've come to see the baby." Sue wondered what baby, then saw Darla behind the woman. It had started to sprinkle rain and the vet had told them to get the newborn filly under shelter lest she get pneumonia. Sue joined Darla and her mom to wrestle the filly and mare into the barn. It took all three of them to get this bucking filly inside.

Sue graduated from high school in 1973 and that fall left for Texas to attend Jacksonville Baptist College in Jacksonville, Texas. She chose JBC because her high school friend Debbie Chandler lived there. Debbie and her family had moved there at the end of their junior year.

*Jesus wants to reveal Himself in your trial.*

May 1974 getting ready to leave for Good News Club in a nearby neighborhood, I heard Harvey, our German Shepherd dog, barking in the front yard. When I opened the front door, I saw a man in our driveway with Harvey barking at him. I called Harvey inside and then asked the man what he wanted. He said, "I thought you might need some help with your horse" pointing towards the pasture. I looked toward our pasture and saw Gypsy caught in the barbed wire fence and lying on the ground. The man and I walked over to where the horse was lying and as soon as the man got near Gypsy, she started kicking at him. I prayed that the man would not be injured. Then he saw that the barbed wire was stuck between one of her hoofs and the horseshoe. He said if I had a wire cutter, he would cut that wire and set her free. I went for the wire cutter, and he approached Gypsy. I kept praying for the man's safety. He was able to cut the wire and free Gypsy's hoof. When Gypsy was freed, she came up outside of the pasture into our front yard. The man was trying to hold her while I fetched her halter. By the time I returned to the front yard, Gypsy had dragged the man across the yard. Finally, he was able to get the halter on the horse, led her to the pasture gate and put her back into the pasture. As we were walking back towards his car, I then saw the plate on his front bumper which read, "Christ is the Answer." I found out that he was a pastor and was driving by when he noticed the horse in trouble.

I was late getting to the Good News Club that day, but my co-workers kept the kids busy reciting their memory verses. I explained why I was late and added I had lived Isaiah 65:24, "It will also come to pass that before they call, I will answer; and while they are still speaking, I will hear." Before I even knew I needed help, God had sent the needed help, and while I was praying for the man's safety, God heard and answered that prayer too. I love it when He shows me His living Word in action.

*Faithful devotion accepts that trials and tests are a when and not an if in life.*

Linda graduated high school in 1974 after completing her junior year. The high school began allowing students who had the appropriate number of credits to graduate early. We then moved from Indianapolis to Smithville, Indiana, a short drive south of Bloomington, the home of Indiana University.

The Smithville property was purchased by us and a group of friends who had invested in Brookhaven Enterprises hoping to build a theme park resort on the land. It was near Lake Monroe. Rex also began another development near this lake as a campground. He enjoyed investing and developing land projects. His work with the Indiana Manufacturing Housing Association dealing with all types of zoning issues and permitting gave him expertise in land acquisition and development, but also a lot of personal debt for us.

That summer the Ben Davis High School Band of Indianapolis, of which Linda was a member playing the baritone horn, was invited to compete in the World Festival of Music in Kerkrade, Holland. Rex, Sue, Linda and I took the European tour with the High School band flying from Chicago to Amsterdam. After sightseeing there we went on to Kerkrade for the Music Festival. Their band won first place in the Marching Band Division competing with 19 other nations. They won second place in the Concert Band Division. Their band did not compete in the Show Band competition won by a Canadian band.

There were 220 of us on this European tour. We were transported in three double deck buses which were all driven by Germans. The band instruments and uniforms were in a truck following the caravan.

The $900 per person cost covered airfare, all ground transportation in Europe, all lodging and meals for three and one-half weeks touring eight countries (Holland, Germany, Switzerland, Lichtenstein, Austria, Italy, Monaco and France). You didn't need any cash unless you wanted to shop or buy snacks and drinks. It was my first overseas travel at age 45. Prior to the trip I had only been out of the USA to visit both Canada and Mexico. I really enjoyed seeing the antiquity of the European civilization but did not enter any country of my ancestry (England, Ireland, Denmark or Norway).

The band also gave concerts in Innsbruck, Austria; Venice, Italy; Nice, France; and under the Eiffel Tower in Paris. We flew out of Paris to Chicago on our return to America.

*Is there good in your trials?*

August 1974, Rex and I drove Linda to Los Angeles Baptist College located in Newhall, California north of Los Angeles to begin her freshman year. After we left Linda at college Rex and I proceeded north to Yosemite National Park and then eastward back to Indiana.

Christmas 1974, Linda flew to Texas from California and Rex and I drove from Indiana to Tyler, Texas to spend time with Sue who remained in Tyler after her first year of college in nearby Jacksonville, Texas. Sue had us bring new contact lenses from her eye doctor in Indianapolis. We four were staying in a motel room as Sue had a roommate in a small mobile home which didn't have enough room for us.

On Christmas Eve, we were preparing to attend Sue's church for a special service. Sue asked where her contacts were that she had left on the desk in the room wrapped in blue tissue paper. (You could do that with hard contact lenses.) That put me in a panic as I had cleaned the room and thrown that "blue tissue" into the trash can. I ran up to the motel office and asked where they dumped the trash. The lady pointed to a big trash dumpster behind a nearby restaurant. It was twilight and starting to sprinkle. I leaned over the big dumpster and started praying asking God to show me where the contact lenses were in all the trash. The dumpster had plenty of garbage, but I did spot a "speck" of blue. Checked it out – and sure enough – God heard my prayer and directed my vision to the contacts. What a faithful God!

July 14, 1975, I began working at Hoosier Energy Rural Electric Company which generated electricity for all the rural areas in the southern half of the State of Indiana. I started as an Accounts Payable Clerk. In less than three years I was promoted to a Junior Accountant position where I took care of the billing to 220 substations, calculated the fuel energy surcharge which was audited every three months by the Public Service Commission of Indiana, did daily weighted coal averages on two power plants for BTUs, sulfur, ash, before and after burn and prepared monthly records for the federal government. I sent these monthly reports consisting of several pages for the two separate coal-fired power plants to the Rural Electric Administration in Washington, D.C. There was a list of 40 different responsibilities for me to complete every month as there were other accounts processed as well. We had three annual audits: an internal audit, a federal audit, and an audit for the State of Indiana. The first round of audits after my employment I realized what the auditors wanted. Thereafter I was prepared each year for their arrival with all the documents copied in folders ready when asked. I took immense pride in being prepared for these audits.

Fall of 1975, Linda entered Baylor University in Waco, Texas as Los Angeles Baptist College (now known as the Master's College) did not have the courses she needed for nursing. She had one year on the Waco campus, as her junior and senior years were at Baylor School of Nursing in Dallas, Texas.

*Remember what matters in life.*

Sue married Rick Cochran on July 11, 1976. They had eloped and when they told us of their marriage, I stated, "now, I've reaped everything I've sown." Rex and I had left Florida and eloped to marry in Texas. On October 20, 1977, we were presented with our first grandchild – a grandson, whom they named Jeremiah. Rick and Sue had moved their mobile home to Bloomington from Indianapolis but were unable to hook up the utilities before the ground froze. They ended up living in the farmhouse with Rex and me on the Brookhaven Enterprise property when Jeremiah was born. The night he was born Rex and I and two others were planning to leave Bloomington and drive straight through to Dallas, Texas to meet with Linda for Baylor's Homecoming. Sue was distressed that we were leaving town as she was past her due date. To calm her, we clarified that if she were in labor before time to leave, we would stay until the baby was born. Sure enough, she went into labor. Instead of leaving at 4 p.m. we left at midnight after Jeremiah was born a little after 9 p.m. weighing in at 6 lb. 14 oz. We watched Jeremiah get his first bath and diapers before departing from the hospital. Sue had fared well in that her labor and delivery were not unduly lengthy, and both were thrilled with their new son.

May 1978, Linda graduated from Baylor University in Waco, Texas with her bachelor's degree in nursing. That evening at dinner we met John Gibson for the first time. We had a delightful evening together before Rex and I started the drive back to Indiana that night.

June 1978, Linda went to Austin, Texas to take the State Board exam to become a Registered Nurse. While Linda was on that trip John Gibson read the book she had loaned to him, "Doctar" (doctor in Bengali) by Dr. Vigo Olsen. Dr. Olsen was a medical missionary to Bangladesh with ABWE and around my age. When Linda and I read the book in 1976 we agreed to pray if Linda were to marry, she would marry a man of the caliber of Dr. Olsen. While Linda was in Austin, John devoured the book and decided he wanted to become a medical missionary.

Thanksgiving week of 1978, Rex and I returned to Texas to visit Linda as she asked us to come give her some parental counsel. She realized that she loved John and he had already told her that she was all he would ever want. Nevertheless, she was going to the mission field as a medical missionary with or without a husband, her priority in life.

We had a wonderful week together. John's mother June and sister Ginny came to Dallas from San Antonio also for Thanksgiving. Imagine the conversation around the table with a doctor and three nurses, Linda plus her two roommates. Interesting to say the least.

At the close of the week, Rex and I returned to Indiana. On Sunday night John proposed marriage to Linda. She questioned him at length about God's call on his life because she wanted to be certain they had the same calling. When John finally convinced her that God had called him into medical missions, she said her answer was yes, provided he had the approval of her parents. It took three nights before John was able to reach us by phone. We gave our consent, and the wedding was set for March 3, 1979.

Significant 1979 events: March 3rd was John's and Linda's wedding in Dallas, Texas. Sue wasn't in the bridal party as she was great with child. The weighty commitment before God and tender words of love expressed as John and Linda read their wedding vows, they had written to each another. I was okay until I heard Rex sniffle and then tears leaked from my eyes. On April 4th I turned the big 5 – 0 and celebrated this milestone in my life. May 16th Angela Grace Cochran, my first granddaughter, was born at home. It was a shock as I had spent the night at Rick and Sue's home as Sue started her labor. I was there to care for Jeremiah should they go to the hospital. But Sue's labor stopped, we all went to sleep and I went to work that morning as no more labor pains for Sue. I called their home on my lunch hour only to hear Rick say, "Angela Grace is here. Waiting on a call from the doctor" as he hung up on me. I left work and rushed to the hospital. I asked the nurse where do they take moms with babies not born at the hospital. She said, "you must be the grandmother" and took me to find Sue. The next day, May 17th Anna Louise Moore, my niece drowned in a swimming pool in Ocala, Florida. Her heart was started by electric shock paddles, but she never regained consciousness. Anna's heart continued beating for another 19 days and then she died June 5th, the day before my dad's 75th birthday. June 23rd, Anna's brother Jeff and Lisa Reimer were married. Anna was to have been one of the bridesmaids. Sue's husband Rick was the wedding photographer. John and Linda were on a mission trip in Korea at the time. Thanksgiving week we drove to Florida for Rex's meetings with the landowner about a new land venture along the Rainbow River in Dunnellon, Florida. I returned to Indiana with Sue, Rick and their two children. Rex remained in Florida to work on this new development. What was supposed to last only a few months until Rex got the housing development up and running became a five- and one-half-year commuting marriage.

At Christmas time, Sue, her family and I drove back to Florida to be with Rex and additional family members. Linda and John with his mother June arrived from Texas. We had not seen John and Linda since their wedding. It was an incredibly special Christmas together in Florida.

After that blessed week, Sue, her family and I headed back to the cold north. Rex remained in warm Florida. The Gibsons returned to Texas. What a winter was coming to us in Indiana.

> *"It is the Lord who goes before you. He will be with you; he will not leave you or forsake you. Do not fear or be dismayed."*
>
> *Deuteronomy 31:8*

# RETIRED – RESCUED – REUNITED

## 1980 – 1989

The winter of 1980 in Indiana was frigid with several days below zero. Sue and I with Jeremiah, age 26 months, and Gracie, age seven months, were trying to survive in the old farmhouse on Brookhaven Farm with Rex in warm Florida and Rick working in Terre Haute, Indiana, then "home" on weekends.

I was working full time, going to night school at Ivy Tech one night a week studying Intermediate Accounting (with an abundance of homework), helping with grandkids at night, taking care of Brookhaven Enterprises (I was the bookkeeper.), and selling Fay Swafford Originals at home parties. Well, it about killed me. Early April, Sue and their children moved to Terre Haute with Rick, and I moved into Dottie Huff's home. A renter was found for the old farmhouse.

Dottie was a former missionary to China from 1947 to 1953. She first served in Canton until the Communists took over, then in Hong Kong among the boat people. She maintained her Cantonese language by boarding Cantonese speaking Chinese students attending Indiana University which was within walking distance of her home. She was active in the Women's International Fellowship, which I also became involved in. Dottie was unable to remain in her beloved China because she needed to return to America to care for her mother lasting for nine years.

Dottie invited me to stay at her home because she would see me at church and knew the crushing load I was carrying was far more than I could bear. Had she not rescued me, I don't know how long I would have lasted. I celebrated my 51st birthday in Dottie's home.

Rex still planned to return to his job with HUD in Bloomington, Indiana as he had taken a leave of absence. But the Sateke Village development in Dunnellon, Florida took far longer than anticipated. He could no longer remain on leave from HUD but needed to resign.

Thus began our commuting marriage. We visited each other every other month. Either he would come to Indiana, or I would go to Florida. We both put a lot of mileage on our vehicles and ourselves. It was 885 miles one way.

On May 16, 1981 (Gracie's second birthday), Sue and family moved from Indiana to Ocala, Florida. Rex was staying with my Aunt Sue in Ocala while working on the Sateke Village development.

*Chance Encounter or Divine Appointment?*

In October 1982 Rex and I traveled on vacation with John, Linda and June (John's mother) in a motor home to New England to enjoy the fall foliage. On the way we stopped in Knoxville, Tennessee for the World's Fair. In the ladies' restroom in the RV park where we were camping, I met a lady who was from Oak City, Indiana. In our conversation I told her that I had been in Oak City three weeks earlier attending my friend's funeral. She also attended the funeral of my deceased friend, who was her husband's cousin. We did not meet at the funeral, but a chance meeting in a restroom in Tennessee.

July 1984, Rex met me at Ridgecrest, North Carolina where John and Linda were appointed by the Foreign Mission Board to serve at the Bangalore Baptist Hospital in Bangalore, India with Dr. Rebekah Naylor. Indira Gandi, Prime Minister of India, was assassinated in 1984 and there was plenty of anti-Americanism. For eight months they tried to obtain visas for India to no avail. The

Indian Government gave them a final no. The mission board then proposed they consider serving in Thailand.

*Steadfast – the ability to patiently endure carrying a heavy load.*

I continued to work at Hoosier Energy until August 30, 1985. Before leaving, my boss would have me help the CPA (a lady), a man with his MBA and another man working on his MBA with their accounting problems. I have no college degree, only a high school diploma. However, the boss knew I saw things quickly because of his previous experience with me. They all had far more formal education than I, but I know the God who knows everything. When he would send me to help others, I would pray to God as I walked to their offices, asking Him to reveal the problem to me. Each time as I trusted God according to James 1:5-8, "But if any of you lacks wisdom, let him ask of God, who gives to all men generously and without reproach, and it will be given to him. But let him ask in faith without any doubting, for the one who doubts is like the surf of the sea driven and tossed by the wind. For let not that man expect that he will receive anything from the Lord, being a double-minded man, unstable in all his ways."

His Word is true. As I prayed His Word and believed He would show me, HE DID – every time. I still don't know what their actual problems were because God would take my vision and have me look only to the place on the spreadsheet and point. I merely pointed at the issue, and they fixed it. How great is our GOD!

*Am I letting God use me, or am I trying to use Him?*
*Am I trying to change God or letting Him change me? – Mike Donehey*

I arrived in Dunnellon, Florida on Labor Day 1985. Four days later John and Linda boarded a plane in Gainesville, Florida to begin their first journey to Thailand. They had no difficulty in getting visas to enter Thailand.

September of 1985 John and Linda arrived in Thailand the

day after the attempted military coup. Had Linda not had a severe earache they would have arrived during the attempted coup. They stopped in Hawaii for a few days giving Linda's ear time to heal. Convenient for Linda to travel with her own private physician. We in the States heard nothing from them for three weeks. Not knowing kept us praying non-stop as the TV news in America showed the tanks and guns in Bangkok, where the photographer was killed taking the news reel.

Retiring at age 56 and moving back to Florida I thought about going to college and getting a degree in Education so I could teach in our Church's Christian school. Unfortunately, every month someone in my family needed me as their caregiver.

In the process of retiring, I constantly thought about ways to get us out of debt, closing the Brookhaven Enterprises corporation (which never materialized), and paying off the mortgage on our home in Sateke Village. I spent many years of sleepless nights and days pondering, figuring and refiguring means to accomplish these things. Another example of how my mind calculates. This time a frustrating and persistent nag in my numbers brain and prayers to no avail. Or so I thought, until God showed me these words from a poem titled "Broken Dreams".

> At last I snatched them back and cried,
> "How can You be so slow" –
> "My child," He said,
> "What could I do?
> You never did let go."

The poem shocked me into reality. What I gave to God in prayer, then took back through my figuring and refiguring perpetuated a restless mind. I learned to let go and let God manage all the details of closing Brookhaven Enterprises and the pay-off of our mortgage. Praise the Lord for lessons learned and experiencing His hand at work.

*Pursue the opportunity to bless others.*

On Sue and Rick's eleventh wedding anniversary, July 11, 1986, my sister Nellie had cancer surgery in Miami. I was with Nellie in Miami and friends took Rex for cataract surgery at St. Luke's Eye Institute the same day. I couldn't be in two places at once. Grateful for friends stepping in to help us.

In August 1986, Nellie left Miami, Florida after living there her entire life to come live with Rex and me in Dunnellon. She retired after working 42 consecutive years for Western Union. Nellie recovered from her cancer surgery and lived 17 years at our home in Dunnellon.

*No matter where you are there is hope.*

Linda asked Rex and I early in 1986 to plan on touring Israel with them in October. In checking airfares, the Jordanian airline Alia was a hundred dollars cheaper than flying El Al, the Israeli airline. We applied for visas to Jordan through the Jordanian Embassy in Washington, D.C. We received not only the visas, but literature and information about entering Jordan. We were warned never to say the name "Israel" while in their country as our safety could not be guaranteed if uttered that "name." Should we care to visit Israel, we had to ask for permission to cross the border to tour the West Bank. If planning to return to Jordan from the "West Bank," we were not to bring any souvenir items or magazines with the name "Israel" on it. Also, if we had an Israeli stamp in our passport, we would not be allowed to enter their country. We were forewarned. With visas in hand, we purchased our tickets with Alia airlines early for the $100 discount per ticket given.

October 1986, Rex and I flew to Ammon, Jordan where we met John, Linda and Vera, who had flown in from Thailand. They arrived five hours before us and had already talked with a tour agent about seeing Petra upon our return from Israel to Jordan.

After our arrival we also spoke with agent about visiting Petra. Rex specifically wanted to see Petra as he had already lived and fought in Israel during their War for Independence in 1948 before we were married. John had booked a time share at the Commodore Hotel beside the Mediterranean Sea in Tel Aviv for a full week. Our previously scheduled flights were booked for the day after we leaving Israel returning to Ammon to board our flight with no lay over in Jordan. The tour agent suggested he could talk with the airline to find out if we could use our tickets two days later to give us time to tour Petra.

When the agent returned, he assured us that our tickets on Alia, the Jordanian airline, would be usable two days later than scheduled.

The following morning the tour agent had a taxi at the hotel to take us to the border between Israel and Jordan at the Allenby Bridge over the Jordan River which divides the two countries. We took the shuttle bus across Allenby Bridge. As it was the dry season, the river was so narrow that I missed seeing it. Both countries had gun towers overlooking the Allenby Bridge where they kept guns aimed at each other.

We rented a car and made our daily travel plans using a good guidebook. It is the most thrilling trip I have ever taken in my lifetime going to the places where Jesus lived and walked. We had a glorious week in Israel going to the places we have read about in the Bible. Before entering Bethlehem, we saw Rachel's tomb. After visiting the place of Jesus' birth in Bethlehem we went outside of the city to Shepherds' Field on a moonlit night. What an impressive moment. Linda and I prayed at the Wailing Wall in Jerusalem on the Day of Yom Kippur. We saw Joseph's tomb and Jacob's well where we read the story of the Samaritan woman who met Jesus at the well. We went to "Gordon's Tomb" outside the old city of Jerusalem near the Jaffe Gate where we sat in the garden and read the accounts of the resurrection. This was my favorite spot in all of Israel. Spent time at the synagogue ruins of Capernaum. Ate fish at Peter's Perch by the Sea of Galilee and watched the fishers casting their nets into the lake while we dined. I put my feet in the Mediterranean Sea, Sea of Galilee, Jordan River and entered the waters of the Dead Sea. You cannot sink because of the dense minerals in the Dead Sea, a strange sensation indeed.

After our wonderful week in Israel, we headed back to passport and customs on the Israeli side of the border. Both countries charge an exit tax and play the same border game. Israel knows you cannot reenter Jordan with an Israeli stamp in your passport. Instead, they stamp an official paper that will fit in your passport which is removed when you exit Israel.

We crossed the Jordan River on a shuttle that was also carrying a Danish couple. They were checking in at passport and customs ahead of us. The Jordanians found beautiful tourist magazines of Israel in their luggage with the "hated name" Israel emblazoned on them. The customs agents went into a rage, tearing the covers off then stomping on the magazines with their feet. I couldn't believe my eyes seeing grown men behaving like they did. Because we had been forewarned so we were not guilty, however, the custom agent decided to confiscate John's camcorder he had recently purchased in the USA. The agent said he could not bring Israeli products into Jordan. John produced his sales receipt showing he had purchased the camcorder in America. John towering over him with the receipt the agent gave the camcorder back.

The tour agency's driver waited for us at the border and took us to Petra. We rode on horseback into Petra with two guides leading. Linda is the only person who has ever succeeded in getting her dad on a horse and this was the second time. The first was during our trip in 1982 while in Vermont. Petra was a remarkably interesting place, and the guide gave us a detailed history of the people who had lived there.

We returned to Ammon to the same hotel we had stayed in before going to Israel. The following day John, Linda and Vera flew back to Thailand. The flight to Kennedy airport on Long Island, New York wasn't departing for another day. Rex and I spent another night in Ammon. The morning of our departure we left early by taxi to go to the airport far outside the city of Ammon. When presenting our tickets at the counter we were informed they had expired, and we could not use them. Rex explained to the ticket agent about the tour agent checking with their airline and was assured that our tickets would be good two days later if we stayed in Jordan to tour Petra. We had only one $20 American Express Travelers Check with no credit card or check book on us. The man made a phone call and soon two men appeared taking Rex with them. He was in possession of the one remaining Travelers Check.

As I stared at the big clock on the wall, I earnestly prayed that God would somehow get us on that flight to Kennedy Airport. Every time the ticket agent wasn't busy, he would walk over to me and say we had made a big mistake and shouldn't have done what we did. Finally, he said it one time too many. I asked him, "Are you telling me that we are not to trust your countrymen?" After that, he stayed away from me. As the hands on the clock were getting closer to departure time, I kept on asking God to intervene. The two men appeared with Rex instructing the ticket agent to let us board the plane. I wasn't going to ask Rex how that happened in anybody's hearing as I didn't want them to change their minds for any reason.

Both of us were body searched before being allowed to board the plane. A first for me but happen again later in Nepal.

After we were airborne and no longer over Jordanian airspace, I asked Rex, "How did we get out?" He explained to the airline officials who took him away our story that the tour agent had assured us we could use the tickets. Thankfully, Rex had the business card of the tour agent. The airline officials called the tour agent and had him come to the airport. In facing Rex, he agreed that the promise had been made. A decision was reached. We were allowed to use our tickets provided we reimbursed the airline the $200 ($100 each) discount we had received for purchasing our tickets five months in advance. The big problem was we only had that $20 Travelers Check. The tour agent paid the airline the $200 since Rex promised that he would reimburse the $200 once he was back home and could mail him a check. Thankfully, the tour agent trusted Rex to pay.

I was full of praise and thanksgiving to God for answering my prayer that I asked God to show me His rainbow since I had heard that a rainbow seen from above is a perfect circle. As soon as I made my request, I looked out the window and saw His rainbow over the

Danube River. It was a perfect rainbow-colored circle. I have flown round trips to and from Asia seven times and crossed the Atlantic round trips three times and that is the only time I have seen a rainbow from above – only when I asked God to show it. How near He is to those who call upon Him.

*Heaven is my home; I'm just here recruiting.*

Back in Florida I became involved with Backyard Bible Clubs, but we met in the church rather than in someone's backyard. Young people are such a joy. Sherry McClain, my prayer partner in Dunnellon, and I made a good team.

One day while cooking on our electric stove, Rex put a Pyrex dish on the burner beside me. He did not know that it had recently been used and was hot. In a brief time, the dish exploded while I was standing beside it. There were burns in the linoleum on the floor and glass everywhere near me, yet not one piece of glass touched my body. How real His Word is, "The Lord is my strength and my shield; my heart trusts in Him, and I am helped; therefore my heart exults, and with my song I shall thank Him."

In 1987, Sue's and Rick's 11-year marriage failed, and Sue became a single mom. It was an exceedingly tough time, but the Lord's mercies never failed. Rex and I became part-time parents to Jeremiah and Gracie, helping fill some of the void with Rick's departure from the family.

February 1988, I made my first trip to Thailand. I was only there long enough to obtain a visa to enter Nepal with Linda and Kathy to take a care package to fellow believers doing medical work in Nepal. We saw Mount Everest from the airplane high above the clouds, along with other high mountain peaks. On the ground you could rarely see the peaks because they were usually above the clouds.

The day after our arrival in Nepal, we took a 13-hour bus ride, jammed with humanity, to reach our destination which was less than 200 kilometers. There never was a restroom available during the entire trip. Periodically the bus would stop, and people would get off to use the hillside or the ditch beside the road as a restroom. Linda and I never did. We arrived after dark and then had a 20-minute walk up to their home on a trail that everyone and every animal "used." It wasn't safe to place your foot anywhere in Nepal without looking where you stepped. In the dark five of us walked with only two flashlights to show us anything on the trail.

Our first question when entering their home, "Where's the bathroom?" Nothing like an American bathroom. We showered under a bucket with a spicket and a hole in the floor.

After visiting their neighbors and ministry work for two days, we took a bus to Pokhara to trek in the Annapurna range (four peaks over 25,000 feet), a three-day trek. Since the agency where we had to get a trekker permit wanted a bribe, we lost a day. We decided that was just as well because two days were enough trekking. We stayed overnight in a private residence with no electricity or plumbing. The bathroom was a curtained place down a path. Overnight sleeping was in a "stall" on the second floor which you accessed by climbing a ladder. The three of us slept (using that word loosely) in the same "bed" as they called it. Only one side of the "bed" didn't touch either a wall or the door. The lock was a nail in a piece of wood for you to turn to block the door.

The following morning, I started out on the trail alone heading back the way we had come (we had made nearly half of the three-day trek in one day). When Linda returned from the "bathroom" she asked Kathy where I was. Kathy explained that I was getting a head start up the trail alone. Linda freaked out as the owner where we had stayed apologized for the dog barking considerably during the night stating the dog only did that when a tiger was nearby. She was terrified that she would find the tiger having her mother for breakfast. She quickly caught up with me and was relieved that I wasn't with the tiger. We talked for a while and still Kathy had not caught up with us as she was waiting for our two porters to finish their breakfast. Kathy felt if she left ahead of them, we would never see our gear again. After waiting and praying for God's protection, I forged on alone while Linda waited there for Kathy and the porters to join her. Not long afterward we were all together again.

Back at a lodge in Pokhara, we all had a good shower and shampoo. The most appreciated shower in a lifetime. The next day we took the bus back to Kathmandu for our flight back to Bangkok, a two-hour forty-minute flight. Here we were body searched before boarding the plane.

John met us in Bangkok to take a vacation in the south of Thailand. We first went to Hua Hin and stayed at the Juniper Tree (my favorite spot in all of Thailand). Next, we went to Krabi where we stayed with friends. We took a boat to the Phi Phi Islands and spent two nights there. After that we drove to Phuket Island where went snorkeling in the Andaman Sea which was warm like bathwater. I like warm water, so it was delightful.

After vacation we went to Bangkla, sixty miles due east of Bangkok, to their home. John and Linda worked at the Bangkla Baptist Hospital. Linda, a nurse anesthetist, would put a patient to sleep, and John would perform the needed procedure. They were a team. This was B.C. (before children), but that would change wonderfully.

April 4, 1989, I had my 60th birthday. It came so soon in life.

> "O LORD, make me know my end
> and what is the measure of my days;
> let me know how fleeting I am!
> Psalm 39:4

In August 1989, our new pastor Rev. Dwayne Kitchens came. I was elected Church treasurer just before his arrival (a volunteer job without pay). Another effective use of my number's skill.

September 1989, John and Linda moved to Dunnellon to begin their first furlough (now known as stateside assignment) after serving four years in Thailand. They were expecting their first baby and living next door to us.

Christmas 1989 was terrific for me having both daughters on the same side of the world again.

*"Abide in me, and I in you. As the branch cannot bear fruit by itself,
unless it abides in the vine, neither can you, unless you abide in me.
I am the vine; you are the branches. Whoever abides in me and I in
him, he it is bears much fruit, for apart from me you can do nothing."*

*John 15:4-5*

# THE WORLD AWAITS

## 1990 – 1999

The New Year of 1990 arrived with anticipation of another grandchild, John's and Linda's first child and our third grandchild.

February 9, 1990, I was privileged to be in the delivery room with John and Linda when Kimberly Dawn was born at 8:01 a.m. After she was bathed and presented to her parents my first impression was that she looked highly intelligent. Kimberly was studying her parents with great interest.

It was great fun living next door to the Gibsons while they were on furlough getting to watch Kimberly grow and learn things. When she was seven weeks old, I went with Linda and Kimberly to Des Moines, Iowa as Linda attended classes for Continuing Education credits to maintain her certification in anesthesia. All I had to do for three wonderful days was take care of Kimberly. Des Moines has connecting walkways between downtown buildings that made walking a pleasure as it was still winter. I lost three pounds in three days walking with Kimberly in her stroller. It is amazing the attention you get if you have a baby with you. I felt like I met nearly everyone who worked downtown. One evening Linda insisted I go out to eat and she would stay with Kimberly. Out on my own, no one spoke to me or seemed aware of my presence. Rex always liked to carry our babies in public as he too became the center of attention as people are drawn to babies. And so, I knew I wasn't noticeable at all.

On April 1$^{st}$ on our return flight to Florida we changed planes in Minneapolis where it was snowing. Reminded me of my 26 ½ years in Indiana.

In July Linda had to do more Continuing Education classes. This time in Daytona Beach, Florida just a few hours' drive from home. Again, all I had to do was care for Kimberly, a wonderful occupation. Kimberly was now five months old and very aware of her surroundings, which called for more effort on my part to entertain her.

Later John, Linda, Rex, Kimberly and I took a trip to Helen, Georgia, a tourist town in northeast Georgia which is patterned after a Bavarian Village. It is a fun city with stores selling merchandise from many different countries. Rex's favorite stop was the candy shop. Since then, Sue, Gracie and I have gone there together. I have also gone with three special friends for a time of fellowship plus a couple of other times as well. I guess you can tell I really enjoy visiting Helen, Georgia.

The Gibson's furlough was ending, but before their departure to Thailand, Sue and Michael Schultz married on July 28, 1990, in Tampa, Florida. Rex and I became the "babysitters" of Jeremiah and Gracie during their brief honeymoon. A year later Michael adopted both Jeremiah and Gracie and they became Schultz as well.

August 2, 1990, the day Iraq invaded Kuwait, John, Linda and Kimberly left for Thailand. Gracie cried and cried at the airport because they were taking away her baby cousin. It was certainly harder this time saying good-bye.

*I will cause your name to be remembered in all generations,*
*therefore nations will praise you forever and ever.*
*Psalm 45:17*

January 2, 1991, my dad James Augustus Moore died at age 86 ½ from pneumonia. Thankful that we have a picture of four generations, my dad, me, Linda and baby Kimberly in his hospital bed. My dad loved babies.

### FEAR – False Evidence Appearing Real

January 19, 1991, I landed in Thailand the second time. It was the night the Persian Gulf War started. Soldiers were all over the Bangkok airport. The next day we saw tanks and the military guarding the U.S. Embassy as well as other Embassies.

John was in Malaysia attending the Christian Medical/Dental Symposium where Dr. Paul Brand was the speaker for the week. I stayed with Linda during John's absence. Linda and I took a trip to Hui Hin where the Juniper Tree Lodge is on the coast of Thailand. My favorite place in Thailand and my second time visiting there. Kimberly was almost a year old and came close to falling out of the crib. Linda caught her just in time.

When we returned to Bangkla, where they resided, we received a call telling us to call in the watch dog, lock the gate to the yard and don't go out as a rumor was heard of a 30,000 Baht reward for any Americans. Supachai, the Bangkla Baptist Hospital administrator, was out of town, but was due back the following day. We were advised to not venture out until Supachai checked if there was any truth to the rumor. Thankfully, it was only a rumor. After five weeks in Thailand, I left the day after Kimberly's first birthday to return home.

*There is value to how you live and love others.*

The Gibson's returned again to Florida for their second baby's birth. She was born on November 10, 1992, John's sister Ginny's birthday. I was babysitting with Kimberly while Linda was at the hospital but kept the ham radio on to receive John's updates from the labor room. Over the ham radio I heard Kaitlyn Diane's first cry. The listening ham radio community started calling in to John congratulating them on Katie's birth saying it had been a remarkably interesting morning to be listening.

Kimberly's remark when seeing her sister Katie for the first time, "You can't put marbles in the baby's mouth!" After I had read "Snow White and the Seven Dwarfs" to Kimberly, she looked at her baby sister and quoted from the book, "She's going to be trouble, mark my word!"

Before Kimberly's 3rd birthday, and Katie less than three months old, the Gibsons returned to Thailand in January 1993.

*No deadlines on dreams.*

January 1994, Rex made his first and only trip to Thailand. Both of us were carrying medical equipment in our carry-on luggage for Bangkla Baptist Hospital. But our time was mostly spent in Nan Province in northern Thailand doing mobile medical clinics and/ or caring for Kimberly and Katie while the medical team did the work. While on this trip, Katie spoke her first word, "Eat!" when we entered a restaurant in Chiang Mai after leaving Nan.

This was my first trip to Chiang Mai. Linda took us to see the multitude of factories making various products. I lasted the first day, but that night got extremely sick after eating at McDonalds. (Don't believe I have ever eaten McDonalds again.) Too sick the second day to see any more factories. Linda took her dad and her girls to see more factories while I tried to recover in time to depart that night for Bangkok. Never dreamed that I would one day live in Chiang Mai.

Our return trip to the U.S. was the longest I have ever taken – 44 hours. All was going well until we arrived in San Francisco to change planes for Memphis, Tennessee, the U.S. hub for Northwest Airlines. There had been an ice storm in Memphis leaving the airport with no electricity. All Northwest Airline flights to Memphis were being rerouted on other airlines. After eight hours in the San Francisco airport, we were given a flight on American Airlines into the Dallas/Fort Worth airport. We arrived too late to catch our connecting flight to Tampa, Florida. We ended up spending the night in the airport. The following morning, we caught another flight into Tampa. From Tampa we had a two-hour drive to Dunnellon. We were again carrying medical equipment back to America for repairs.

*If my eyes are on others, myself or desires, I*
*will inevitably lose sight of God.*

In 1994 Sue had emergency eye surgery at 10 p.m. on a Saturday night in Tampa, Florida. She had just returned from a trip with a black curtain coming over her vision. She went to a retinal specialist, and he sent her straight to the hospital as the retina was detaching from the back of her eye. The doctor had to stitch a "buckle" on the back of her eye to reattach the retina. Michael took care of her that weekend and I went down on Monday to watch over Sue while Michael was at work. Driving back to Dunnellon later in the week, I noticed when a car passed me it disappeared from my vision after passing. I began to check my eyes separately by the highway signs as I drove past. The signs took the shape of an hourglass when checking my right eye. My left eye saw a normal road sign.

Upon arrival home I immediately called my eye doctor to request an appointment in the morning. My eye doctor, Dr. Warren, was scheduled for surgeries and would be a long wait for an appointment with him. I asked for an appointment with someone else in the group explaining what I had discovered about the vision in my right eye. My appointment the following morning, the doctor discovered a hole in the center of my macula which was why I lost central vision. He recommended a doctor in Daytona Beach who did the necessary surgery to correct it as no local doctor could perform the surgery necessary to repair the macula. Nellie and I drove to Daytona Beach to see this recommended doctor and he spent his time with me explaining and showing all that was needed to correct it. I left having no peace about that doctor doing the surgery.

September 13, 1994, Adele had a mastectomy. Eight days later I had a breast biopsy, but by God's grace I didn't have cancer. This was Adele's second bout with cancer as years before she had ovarian cancer. Thankfully, it was detected early, had the necessary surgery, but did not have to endure chemotherapy or radiation.

Adele told me about Dr. H. Logan Brooks in Tallahassee, Florida who did the kind of surgery my eye needed. Made an appointment with Dr. Brooks and went to see him. Immediately I felt a real peace about this Christian doctor who was highly recommended by Adele's doctor in Georgia. The surgery was performed on the Monday following Thanksgiving Day in 1994. The fluid was removed from my right eye and a gas replaced it. The recovery meant keeping my face parallel to the floor for three and one-half weeks so the gas could press the hole closed while the eye replenished its fluid. I would lie across my bed and sleep on my stomach with my face in a "donut" pillow braced between the bed and a piano bench so I could breathe. I could walk around if I kept my face down parallel to the floor. I could eat in this same facial positioning, without raising my head. After the recovery time was up, I returned to the surgeon for a checkup. He wondered if I was going to be able to straighten up after that long, but diligently doing so brought healing as the hole had closed. However, the gas had not totally dissipated, and I was instructed not to lie on my back because doing so would allow the gas to bubble up under the iris and blind me. To be certain I didn't roll onto my back while asleep, I put a baseball in an athletic sock and pinned it to the back of my sleepwear as I couldn't lie on a baseball in the middle of my back. The doctor wasn't pleased that I was soon leaving for Malaysia but laid out my plan to stay off my back while asleep. Anyway, it worked, and I visually saw the last bubble of gas exit out of my eye while in Malaysia.

*God wants the world to see your faith in the midst of your trials.*

January 1995 I was heading back to Asia for the fourth time. Linda asked me to accompany her to the medical symposium at White Sands, Port Dickson, on the Malacca Straits off the west coast of Malaysia to take care of Kimberly and Katie while both she and John attended classes for their continuing education credits to remain certified. John flew ahead of us to Kuala Lumpur. Linda, the girls and I flew to Singapore for Linda to get a doctor's appointment on our return through Singapore to Thailand. She needed to see an ear specialist. We stayed at the Seventh Day Adventist Guest House that night. We also met with Harry, the son of a member of my home church, as I was delivering gifts between father and son. We exchanged goods and enjoyed a good visit.

The following morning, we traveled for five hours by train into Malaysia. Since Linda knew the particulars of our trip, I didn't bother to ask for details. Never again. When it was time to get off the train, Linda took Katie in her car seat. Kimberly was to follow her mother off the train, and I was to get our luggage off. Kimberly did not keep up with her mother. By the time Kimberly and I got to the steps to get off the conductor stopped us. We could not exit as the train was departing. And depart it did. Linda had my purse with my passport and money. I didn't know where I was in Malaysia, nor our destination. Linda had her back to the train trying to hire a taxi and was oblivious to the train departing with her mother and child.

My mind raced ahead to the possibilities, and I started screaming at the top of my lungs, "Stop the train, Stop the train, I have to get off!!" I kept yelling until the conductor pulled the cord and the train stopped to let this screaming woman and bewildered child off a few hundred feet down the tracks. Linda missed it all.

How thankful I am that the conductor pulled the cord as a terrified passenger not knowing where we were and unaware of the hour-long taxi ride to White Sands. The Lord heard my desperate cry and helped me. I have since made it a point to know all travel plans and pertinent travel arrangements.

As we were leaving White Sands, Clyde Meador came for some meetings. He handed Linda the key to his apartment in Singapore where we would stay while Linda had her appointment with the ear specialist. In the lobby of that building there was a sign on the wall by the elevators, "There has been some vandalism in the parking lot, remember Michael Fay." After eleven days at White Sands, we went back to Seremban (place of my frantic pleas to stop the train) to board the train. No problem this time as Singapore was the destination.

We had the pleasure of going through the museum of Chinese history in Singapore. It was extremely interesting with wax figures depicting the Japanese taken over and another exhibit of the Japanese surrender after World War II with more figurines.

*Sometimes the way through the trial is what brings the most glory to God.*

We returned to Thailand where I received word from Rex that Jeremiah was in the hospital in Georgia after having an emergency appendectomy. His appendix had ruptured and after major surgery a lot of healing needed to happen. Rex called him every day from Florida while he was hospitalized. They have a strong bond of love.

In 1996 the Gibson family took a six-month furlough in Florida. They arrived in time for Kimberly to start the first grade in Dunnellon Christian School and Katie began K-4. They experienced one semester of school as their mother homeschooled them in Thailand.

December 20, 1996, Gracie married Danny Echols at First Baptist Church of Woodstock, Georgia with both Kimberly and Katie being flower girls in the wedding party. They decided to have the wedding while the Gibson family could be a part of the celebration. It was a beautiful Christian wedding and a blessed marriage.

On Kimberly's and Katie's last day at school as Linda was driving, Katie was fooling around with the car dashboard. Linda was under intense pressure with packing a crate and preparing for their move back to Thailand. She scolded Katie that if she didn't stop giving her so much trouble, she was going to start giving her some trouble. Katie narrowed her eyes and looked at her mom saying, "You are not behaving like an adult!" Later when Linda told me about the conversation, we both laughed hysterically.

We left our home in Dunnellon at 4 a.m. the morning that the Gibson family was departing from the Tampa airport on their return to Thailand. I drove them to the airport but did not get out of my van as I had a bad cold. After I arrived back home, I crawled back into bed to get some much-needed sleep. It didn't happen. John called from the airplane saying that his laptop had been left in the van. He wanted me to have UPS send it to Hawaii where they would spend one night on their way to Thailand. I called UPS and they did not deliver to Hawaii on Saturdays, but the lady who answered the phone told me to call Northwest Airlines (the airline they were using) cargo office in Tampa as they did counter to counter deliveries. After calling cargo I was to bring the laptop to them for that service. Before I left, John called again from Minneapolis airport. I told him that Northwest cargo would deliver the laptop to Honolulu airport. John must go to the airport to pick it up as the service was only from counter to counter in an airport. Then I had to drive the two hours back to Tampa and to cargo. I locked his laptop by moving the dials on its case. When I showed them the laptop, they asked me to open it for inspection. I couldn't as I had locked it and did not know the combination to unlock it. They told me they couldn't put it on an airplane without inspection. I should have known that. I began to plead with them about the circumstances and asked couldn't I take it to the passenger terminal and have them x-ray it. They said no, but as I pleaded more, they decided one of their employees could take it to the passenger terminal and have it x-rayed. Thankfully, they were satisfied after having it scanned that there was no bomb in it. I learn a proper amount of life lessons the hard way.

John was able to pick up his laptop with all of Bangkla Baptist Hospital data on it at the airport in Honolulu the one day they were in Hawaii and travel on to Thailand.

*Our lives are not meant to be lived for pleasure in this world,*
*but for joys in the next.*

Sue's church, First Baptist Church of Woodstock, Georgia, offered a one-day seminar on "What the Bible Says About Healthy Living" taught by Dr. Rex Russell. It was at this seminar I made friends with Bonnie Morrell, who introduced me to Sue Becker and her business. Bread Beckers business instructed people on how to mill your own grains making homemade, healthy bread. I was hooked. On my birthday in 1998 Sue Becker came to First Baptist Church of Dunnellon, Florida demonstrated bread making with fresh milled grains. I became the first point of contact for Sue's customers in Florida as her business grew. Bread Beckers now own and operate a store in Woodstock, Georgia with a large online presence as well.

*Faith is tested through trials not produced by trials.*

In May 1998 Rex had a stroke. He refused medical care. It didn't disable him, but from that time forward he was going downhill.

That summer both my brothers went to Thailand to help with the construction of the Chiang Klong Baptist Clinic. They had borrowed "my" car to drive to San Francisco where they would fly to Thailand. I say, "my" car, as legally it was considered thus, but when purchased, I gave the car to God. Good thing I had because the brothers' last night before flying to Asia was spent at a motel in northern California where the key had been left in the door of the car. All a thief had to do was open the car and drive off as the key was visibly available. But the car was still there the following morning with the key still in the keyhole. While they were driving north on I-5 towards San Francisco, several cars had blown their horns at them. Finally, one driver riding alongside the vehicle spoke to my brother after he rolled the window down. The other driver said that the car key was hanging from the trunk lock. Both brothers had a key to the car. Never knew which one left the key in the car, maybe they each did it once.

Later, Bob's wife Vivian and I drove to San Francisco to meet them at the airport upon their return from Thailand. We both were on time and happily drove together to Oakland where "my" car was parked at our nephew Jeff's sister-in-law's home. We spent two days in San Francisco enjoying the sights and then headed north to the California Redwoods. After Marvin showed us the Redwoods, we parted company. Bob and Vivian headed north up the Oregon coast and Marvin and I headed east towards home. We spent our first night in Provo, Utah and from there drove straight through to Acworth, Georgia which was around 2,000 miles. It took two days and a night to do so. We took turns driving. He was ready to be home, but I insisted we were to stop in Georgia to see my first great grandchild, Nathan Michael Echols, born August 19, 1998, before proceeding to Florida. He had been born while I was traveling out west.

*When I fail to praise God, I'm acting against my created purpose.*

On Easter Sunday, April 4, 1999, I celebrated my 70th birthday. I had known for decades that if I lived until my 70th birthday that it would come on Easter Sunday. As a young person I had often wondered if I would live that long. Now, I've discovered that my 81st birthday will occur on Easter Sunday 2010. Only God knows if I will be around then or not, but He has already given me many years beyond a life span. What a journey it has been.

Sue planned a lovely birthday party for me at my brother Marvin's home in Ocala, Florida on Saturday, April 3rd. Had to leave my birthday party early to drive to Tampa to pick up Nellie and her friend returning from New York City where they had enjoyed the Smithsonian Metropolitan Opera tour. For a week following that tour about all I heard out of my sister was about the tour.

That Easter Sunday, Sue had a dozen yellow roses on the communion table at church in celebration of my 70th birthday. Beautiful!

Lila as a teenager      Rex, Lila and Pamela Sue

Lila with Pamela Sue      Rex, Lila, Pamela Sue and
Linda Diane (infant)

Lila with siblings: Bobby, Nellie, Marvin, Lila and Thelma Adele

Lila with her great-grandchildren: Daniel and Nathan (back row) Brianna, Jewel, Jonah, Lila and Jonathan

Lila in Mongolia

Lila at her desk working in Thailand

Lila welcomed home at Atlanta
International Airport

Kisses and much love shared
with granddaughter Kimberly

Lila sharing a kiss with great-great-
granddaughter Izzy.

Lila playing Rummikub

# DEATH, DISEASE AND DELIGHTFUL COMPANY

## 2000 – 2009

According to the dooms day sayers, all systems run by computers were to crash at midnight when the clock rolled over to January 1, 2000! Nevertheless, the world is still in orbit and God is still in control.

This year did not start out with a bang, but the decade had just begun and there would be plenty of experiences worth noting.

On May 8th I took Rex to the VA hospital in Gainesville, Florida after his collapse at home. I was sick first, but he caught what I had. That morning while getting Rex into the shower to bathe him, his weak legs gave way, and he went to the floor - half in the shower and half out. Nellie and I together could not lift him. I called the church and the new youth pastor (his first day on the job) with our young Dunnellon Christian School Principal came to the house, lifted him and set him where I could bathe and dress him. Then the men put him into the car. Nellie and I took him on to the hospital. He was dehydrated. The hospital admitted him and administered an IV which he kept trying to remove. Rex thought removing the IV might hurry his death as he longed for heaven.

Thus began my daily commute to the hospital (90 miles round

trip). The doctor's wanted to give Rex a feeding tube. Both Rex and I had Living Wills which stated we did not want anything done to keep us alive if we were in a terminal condition. However, I wanted to find out how our daughters felt and did not want to make any decision with which they did not agree. This began the three-way conversation with both daughters, one in north Georgia and the other in Thailand. The three of us agreed that we should honor his request and refuse the feeding tube. They put him back on IV treatment for another 24 hours after which he was able to take food orally again.

On May 16th, Gracie's 21st birthday, Rex was taken to an Ocala rehab center to see if he could regain enough strength to walk again. He was nearer family and others could visit him as well. He remained there for two months before being released.

The day Rex checked out of rehab, we drove directly from there to Sue's home in Acworth, Georgia, a six-hour trip. The Gibsons were due in the USA on August 1st and would spend their furlough in Bimble, Kentucky – six miles east of Barbourville. They wanted Rex and me to stay with them while they were in the States. We arrived in Bimble on Sunday September 13th after attending services to hear Henry Blackaby speak at First Baptist Church Woodstock before our departure for Kentucky. It was a five-hour drive, and we arrived in Bimble to have supper with the Gibson family.

In September, Rex became ill again, and Linda lovingly nursed him back to health. With him in that condition it was a great blessing to be living with a doctor and a nurse. Kimberly started 5th grade and Kaitlyn (Katie) was in the 3rd grade in the Bimble public school. They had been homeschooled by their mother all their education except for one semester in Dunnellon Christian School in Florida.

John and Linda received invitations to speak in churches in Florida during the Christmas holidays. We all planned to spend Christmas in Florida. On the 17th of December Linda and her girls went to Gatlinburg, Tennessee to snow ski because John only had one week off from work. I remained "at home" taking care of Rex.

On the 20th Rex got up from the bed where he took his afternoon nap and fell.

Alone I moved him by dragging him across the floor to where he could use his arms to help me get him up. I didn't know he was hurt as he couldn't talk. Together we were able to raise him enough for me to slide his wheelchair beneath him. With him in the wheelchair I decided to exercise on the treadmill where I could keep my eyes on him. I noticed he started sliding down the chair and by the time I reached him we had to start all over again. This time, instead of the wheelchair, I was able to slide a comfortable upholstered chair under him. The chair had an ottoman where I could stretch out his legs. Thankfully, this time he stayed put.

When John came home, he checked Rex's legs and hip joints but did not think he had broken anything. However, when John helped me get him to bed, it was evident that Rex could not bear any weight on his legs. We got him into his wheelchair and took him to the bedroom where John helped prepare him for bed.

The following morning, John checked Rex before leaving for work. He asked me if I wanted Rex to be admitted to the hospital as he knew I couldn't manage him alone. John called for an ambulance and Rex was taken to the Barbourville Hospital. When I arrived not long afterward, his hips had already been x-rayed and indeed he had a broken hip.

John and I with Rex had planned to leave that day to join Linda and the girls in Acworth, Georgia at Sue's house to stay overnight before heading for Florida. That was before Rex was hospitalized. However, we celebrated Christmas the morning of December 22nd as a family at Sue's house before the Gibsons departed for Florida, and I returned to Kentucky alone.

*How we spend our days is how we spend our lives ~ striving or resting.*

I went by the hospital to spend time with Rex before going "home" to an empty house. Christmas Day was spent with Rex at the hospital until it was dark before leaving to retire. When I arrived at the dark empty house, I flipped the switch to turn on the outdoor Christmas tree lights in the backyard. We didn't decorate as we planned to be in Florida. I went to the kitchen to prepare something to eat. While it was heating, I went to the bathroom window to look at the lighted Christmas tree in the backyard. As I gazed out the bathroom window every light on the tree was a lighted CROSS, not a lighted bulb. I looked at each and every light appearing as a CROSS. It seemed as though I heard the Lord say to me, "You are not alone, I am here with you." After a long look I went into the kitchen to eat. Later, I returned to the bathroom (the only room inside the house where you could look out and see this tree) and all the lighted bulbs were now just bulbs – no appearance of crosses. My dear friend Elaine later did a beautiful oil painting of this "tree" with lighted crosses. It is in Sue's home right outside my bedroom where I see it every time I go in and out. Always a beautiful memory of God with me.

On January 2nd, the Gibsons returned to Kentucky with a hospital bed for Rex. The next day we brought Rex home to his private room with a view and his own hospital bed. He continued to go downhill and on January 11th we knew his time on earth was nearing an end. Sue was on her way to see her dad, but at 10:15 p.m. she called to inform us that her vehicle's water pump stopped working and dumped all the water from the engine at a service station in Clinton, Tennessee ninety miles away. Since Linda said that it was possible Rex might go into convulsions, she thought I should be the one to fetch Sue. Plus, she and John would know what to do.

By the time I reached Sue after 11 p.m., Rex had died in Bimble, Kentucky. We returned by 1 a.m. but funeral personnel had not picked up his body. It was nearly 3 a.m. by the time they came. The owner of the funeral home was a member of the church we had been attending. They were truly kind.

*You cannot rest in a place you're not or
wishing you were somewhere else.*

Sue and Linda thought it would be good to have his funeral in Bloomington, Indiana at the church where we had been members for several years. It was a short drive for both of his brothers in Indiana. Also, Bloomington was nearer for his siblings and other family to come since they were in Missouri, Illinois, Wisconsin and New Jersey. Our burial plots are in Florida and knowing it would be too long a journey for them to take in the winter weather this seemed a satisfactory solution. Pastor Doug Schroeder knew both Rex and me very well and agreed to have the funeral at 2 p.m. on Sunday afternoon at Emmanual Baptist Church.

Early Sunday morning, January 14, 2001, we picked up Rex's casket at the funeral home in Kentucky with a travel permit to transport a dead body and drove 300 miles to Bloomington, Indiana on snowy roads. We arrived early enough for the men of the church to carry his casket inside where a stand loaned from a local funeral home was set to hold Rex's casket. After a lovely service, the women of Emmanuel had a meal prepared for the family members which numbered close to fifty.

At 5 p.m., John and I started our drive to Michael and Sue's home in Acworth, Georgia with Rex's casket remaining in the van in their garage overnight. Others from my side of the family had to go back to Barbourville, Kentucky and pick up a vehicle left there and then proceed to Georgia. We needed to get part of the trip behind us as our church in Dunnellon, Florida where Rex's and my memberships were, prepared a memorial service at 7 p.m. on Monday, January 15th. We were all shocked when the minister during the service played a recording of Rex saying, "You're the man. You're the man. I want you to speak at my funeral." when preplanning his funeral service. It was a hilarious moment hearing Rex speak at his own funeral.

Tuesday morning, we took his casket to Good Shepherd Memorial Gardens in Ocala, Florida for burial. The same two men who had picked Rex up from the floor (his last day in his own home) plus two more men from the church met us at the cemetery. They served as pallbearers taking his casket from the van to the burial plot. After our family graveside goodbyes, Linda, Sue and I headed north to Acworth, Georgia. Sue had to return to work and Linda's husband and children were already in Kentucky due to John's work and the girls' schooling.

Linda and I stayed overnight at Sue's home and left the next morning to return to Kentucky. We stopped at the Social Security Administration office in Kentucky to report Rex's death. During the interview I was asked, "have you been married before?" I responded, "yes." Linda sitting beside me in the interview was in absolute shock, and I told her I would explain. On the ride home I shared about my first marriage and divorce as I feared for my life and hid at my sister Nellie's home to escape his abuse, but her dad had forbidden me to tell anyone because that would disqualify him to serve in the church. Linda said I must tell Sue. I phoned Sue and told her that I had wanted to tell her long ago when she was going through her divorce, but Rex insisted no.

*Never be a prisoner of your past. It was just a lesson, not a life sentence.*

About a month later, Linda suggested that I contact the International Mission Board (IMB) for service. She was the one who had the IMB mail me the initial application. After I sent the initial application to the Board and was back in Florida when the IMB called to say it was not their policy to send anyone overseas the first year after the death of an immediate family member. I explained to them that my husband had not been able to communicate with me in the past three years and I had done my grieving long before he left this life. His death was a celebration of his homegoing to the Lord.

Next, I was asked by the IMB to have my pastor counsel me. He was to then call the IMB and let them know his evaluation. The following Sunday when I saw Pastor Russ Randall in the hallway at church, I told him about the call from the IMB. He said he would call them in the morning and tell them I was ready to go. So much for counseling.

Then the long application was sent to me. That alone will weed out the fainthearted. The completed application was mailed in and not long afterward I was invited to an interview conference in Richmond, Virginia. During the conference I shared a hotel room with a 22-year-old girl, and I was 72. We have had a good relationship ever since. She went on to Swaziland and is now married and serving in North Africa Middle East (NAME) region for the IMB.

At the interview conference my three choices were: England, Prague or Chiang Mai, in that order. I was appointed to England to serve in the NAME office of finance.

July 30th, I reported to Missionary Learning Center (MLC) for orientation. Greg Holden said it was like trying to take a drink from a fire hydrant. Loved it there and have had forever friends ever since. Among the participants, it was there I met Dr. Greg Greer and his family as they were appointed to work with my son-in-law, Dr. John Gibson, in Thailand.

September 4, 2001, at our commissioning service to the four corners of the earth (over 200 of us), I was handed a message from Dr. Van Williams saying I could not fly (even though I already had my airline tickets in hand to fly to England's Gatwick airport on September 11th) before first having a colonoscopy. My niece Laura managed to get me an appointment for early Monday, September 10th. The previous evening at First Baptist Church of Dunnellon there was a commissioning service for me with gifts from Sunday School classes and classes at Dunnellon Christian School. At least I have the picture of the table full of delicious food even though I could not have one bite as I prepared for my colonoscopy. I also received two money trees loaded with cash totaling over $1,000.

The following morning after the colonoscopy I was informed I had colon cancer and would not be flying anywhere. My next destination was an operating room. What a major detour in my plans.

*Abide means to bear patiently; to remain stable or fixed; to continue in place; to always be actively mindful of God.*

On September 11th as I was driving to Ocala to go to the surgeon's office, I heard on the radio all that was happening in

New York City and Washington, DC as well as the plane crash in Pennsylvania. Thus began my realization of the horror of the attack with so many lives lost. I understood that those victims were suffering far worse than I. Sue drove down after work to be with me during my surgery. She described how eerily the trip had been with no traffic on the roads coming through Atlanta and Interstate signs stating the Atlanta airport closed due to national emergency. As I laid down on the bed that evening, I had Sue feel my abdomen. She was able to feel the cancer tumor.

The following day I entered the hospital for surgery. I was informed by the anesthesiologist that I was anemic, and the surgery could not take place unless I signed papers to receive blood transfusions during surgery. I signed. And that is the last thing I remember until the next day in ICU where I was receiving another blood transfusion. I have no recollection of being moved to ICU or my family visiting with me afterwards though they said I responded like I knew what was going on.

During my week in the hospital the oncologist visited with me recommending that I start chemotherapy a week after my dismissal. I wasn't interested. My sister-in-law Georgia pleaded with me to do it. I had all kinds of different advice from family and friends. All I wanted to do was obey God. Since Dr. Van Williams was the authority over me in my appointment to the mission field – he would determine if or when I could go on to England – I told him that he should decide for me. He was a bit hesitant to do so, therefore, I suggested that he call my son-in-law Dr. John in Thailand and the two of them together decide. They knew each other since 1980 when Dr. Williams was a pediatrician serving with the Bangalore Baptist Hospital in India while John and Linda were there during John's three-month elective while in med school.

The following morning Dr. Williams called me after he had spoken with John in Thailand stating both agreed I should take the chemo. I called the oncologist to set an appointment.

My first chemo treatment was on October 8, 2001, the day of my daughter Linda's 45th birthday. Little did I know on the day she was born how I would be "celebrating" her 45th birthday. I didn't enjoy her birthday that year. For someone who hates needles this was a stark reality for me.

The end of November I received a call from my dear friend Sherry McClain asking me if I could suggest a home for a German exchange student, Kolja Keller. She knew I couldn't invite him into my home but thought I might suggest a good home. After four different families that I thought would make a fine home for the lad, and none could take him in. I told her if later I thought of anyone, I would call her back. Finally, Nellie said, "Well, do what you have to do!" She didn't like the idea, but if a home were not found before Saturday, Kolja would be sent home to Germany. I called Sherry back and said we would take him. This was Tuesday night and I needed to vacate the master bedroom with attached bath for him to move in by Saturday. This gave Kolja private living space and would not interfere with my sister's use of the home.

On Thursday we met Kolja. He looked like a cherub. He moved in on Saturday afternoon with only time to bring in his gear and leave. He played trombone in the high school band and the band was leaving to play a concert out of town that evening. Later that night when he returned, I told him that I went to Sunday school and church in the morning, and he was welcome to join me. He said, "I will go." He felt obligated to me for taking him in as he wanted to stay for the remainder of the school year.

The following morning, I took him to the high school department at church where he attended a class taught by a man who later became an East Asia missionary. The teacher told me afterwards that he couldn't teach the lesson because Kolja kept asking questions. Kolja was not trying to be disruptive. It was the first time he encountered someone who could answer his questions.

After the worship service as we were going out the door Kolja said, "That was a fire and brimstone sermon!" I would not have classified it as such since he didn't even mention hell, but it was a message straight from the Bible. At home, when we were having lunch together, he started asking me questions about God, Jesus and the

Bible. This discussion lasted at least two hours. Each time he asked a question, I gave him no answer from myself, I only read to him from the Bible the portion that answered his question. I explained to him that I hoped he didn't feel pressured about becoming a Christian as that was not something I could do. It is totally a work of God by His Spirit and not by any human. That when God's Spirit spoke to his spirit, how he responded to God determined whether he became a Christian. That discussion took place on December 2nd.

December 9th, Kolja became a child of God and what a beautiful marvel watching him grow in the Lord. During the worst physical trauma in my life, God sent an incredibly special joy to me when he sent Kolja to live with Nellie and me. The night he went forward at the invitation given by the Pastor at the close of the church service, I was standing beside Kolja holding hands. A high school girl that I have known since she was five years old came to the front and held my other hand. I did not know at the time I was holding the hands of the future bride and groom. I missed their wedding because it was a few years later and I was living in Thailand during that joyous occasion.

Kolja's parents came in June to visit and pick up their son. They toured the east coast of America before their departure home to Hamburg, Germany. What a blessing that Kolja's parents Hartmut and Elke-Maria and I have had the opportunity to be together several times. We even spent the afternoon of March 1, 2009, together in Thailand.

*We don't submit our will to God because we don't trust Him completely.*

July 4, 2002, I went with a volunteer mission team from First Baptist Church of Dunnellon, Florida to Thailand to go on mobile clinics and to do dramas in villages in Nan Province. We had a great and rewarding time together. The team was here about 10 days and then flew back to America while I remained another three weeks with my "kids" attending the Buddy Block Annual General Meeting (AGM) with them. It was there I met Gary and Evelyn Harthcock for the first time. I had read about them in the Commission magazine and knew I wanted to meet them. We have been friends ever since. All total I spent five weeks in Thailand before returning to the States for medical check-ups determining if I were cancer free and could head for England at last. Linda was disappointed as she wanted me to travel into China with her and her girls. It wasn't easy to pass up that opportunity. Not knowing that during this decade of my life I would make multiple trips into China, Mongolia, Tibet, Hong Kong and Macau.

All said and done, I did pass the required physicals to go to England fifteen months later than originally planned. In November, about two weeks before my departure, Calvary Baptist Church of Miami, Florida had a reunion in Ocala, Florida of our former youth group and where I saw Al Gammage, Jr., and others that I had not seen in 50 years. I met Al's wife for the first time and saw others that are now with our Lord.

I arrived at Gatwick airport in Surrey County about 8 miles south of the office where I would be working on December 6, 2002. Well, I almost got sent back to the States before I even got out of the airport because I didn't have a return flight booked. They did not want me to enter England without a ticket reservation for my return to America. My boss talked with them and begrudgingly I was given a 6-month visa.

That visa was good until six of us traveled in a van to the Port of Dover and took a ferry boat across the English Channel to Dunkirk, France on Good Friday, April 18, 2003. After Dunkirk we rode into Belgium and stayed in Antwerp with fellow missionaries. The next day we went to Keukenhof Gardens in Holland to see the tulips in all their glory. They were the most brilliant colors I have ever seen in my lifetime. Then back to Antwerp to spend the night. Easter Sunday, we worshiped at the International Church where refugee families from Iraq and Iran attended. After the church service there was a fellowship dinner where we got acquainted with the refugees. Later that afternoon we drove into Germany to a border town as I was the only one on the trip who had previously visited Germany. That night we were back in Antwerp but left the next day to tour a museum in Waregem, West Flanders, Belgium, a town that was under siege by the Germans during World War I for four years. It was where the Flanders poppy fields were located. I bought a card with the poem "In Flanders Field" which was written by a Canadian doctor who was later killed in the War and buried in one of Flanders' Fields. One of the most interesting museums I have ever gone through.

Back across the English Channel arriving at the port of Dover, immigration did not want me to enter even though my "visa" had not expired. It was good until June 2003. The Lord was gracious to me after sharing that my family was arriving from Thailand in July to tour England and Scotland, the land of our ancestry, I was granted another (not welcomed) visa stamp in my passport.

*Every time stuff happens God works it out ~ He comes through.*

Sue informed me that my sister, Nellie, was not doing well and by September I needed to return to Florida as she wasn't expected to live. Sue picked me up at the airport on September 16th. I saw Nellie that night and talked to her, she was too weak to respond, only staring at me. The next afternoon she died two days before her 76th birthday. Her funeral was on her actual birthday, September 19th.

Flying back to Florida to see Nellie, I prayed asking God not to sell my house if He wanted me to remain in Florida. If He wanted me anywhere else, then sell it. I promised the Lord that I would not advertise the house or engage a realtor as I wanted Him to either sell it or not sell it as His direction to me. In less than a week, God sold it for cash at the price I named and was given until December 31st to vacate my home. I had my answer to move on. However, while packing up our home in Sateke Village and giving away most all my earthly possessions I took the time to read the documents and court papers from the Sateke litigation. Rex never shared the details of the lawsuit. It really stung and resurrected some hurt feelings.

I applied with the British Consulate in New York City for a visa to return to England to complete my three-year assignment. The visa was denied. I called the office in England and gave them the news. Then I called the mission board to say I was denied the visa to England but am willing to serve elsewhere if they had a place and need for me. They responded that a job search would be done. Sometime later, the mission board contacted me and asked if I were willing to serve in Thailand. I assured them that was fine with me, and the medical clearance process began again. I was cleared to go and arrived in Chiang Mai, Thailand on June 24, 2004.

The Gibsons and I almost passed each other in the skies as they returned to the USA from Thailand on May 14th, but the Lord did give us a little more than a month before my departure to Thailand.

Besides the office work I did in Chiang Mai I was privileged to travel into China in November 2004 for the first time to the northeast corner. Was it ever cold! My traveling partners were pros, so the trip was a real joy. In China I met the fourth and fifth generations of Gammages for the first time and was able to tell them things about their great grandfather, grandfather and dad (who was born the same year I was born). I have only met one other family that had five living generations – my sister-in-love Georgia Moore, married to my brother Marvin. I didn't know seeing five generations would become true for me too.

During that trip to China, we taught English in a private children's school and a university plus traveled to visit others in different cities to encouraged them. I learned a lot about interacting with internationals when you are the foreigner.

One interaction happened as Christy and I took the train to Changchun. On the train I was able to share the New Testament (since it was bilingual) with people seated in the compartment with me. One man was reading the Book audibly in Mandarin while others began to gather around to listen. After a while, the man looked at me, pointed upward and said, "My God, ten years." After he finished reading the two girls seated next to me took the Book and showed me where the Lord's prayer was in Matthew. When the man who had been reading realized that the girls were familiar with the Book, he started talking with them and an animated conversation ensued. When we reached our destination, the man lowered my heavy suitcase from the compartment overhead and carried it all the way to the platform upstairs. We bid farewell and he is still in my prayers.

Another train ride Christy and I took to Shenyang, Christy was able to share with those in her compartment. After a while she was able to share the Four Spiritual Laws tract with the young man seated next to her. I was seated across the aisle. The man seated across from me seemed interested in what Christy was sharing with her seatmate. I offered him one of the two tracts that I had with me. After reading it he was still interested so I gave him the second tract. He did not choose to keep the tracts, but his face now wore a smile. Christy gave the man next to her the Four Spiritual Laws tract. Then the man asked her for her phone number. Still being cautious she gave him her e-mail address instead.

On both Friday and Saturday during our trip to China, the owner of the school took us to have lunch together after we finished at school. During Saturday's lunch, the owner's brother-in-law, who is a Communist Party member joined us. He had a child in the school where we had taught. He asked the reason for our joy. Christy was able to share how she had had a Buddhist mother and a Marxist dad. She herself had been with her mother to the Buddhist temple and prayed burning incense. However, she said she would come out of the temple just as empty as she had been going inside. She thought that perhaps her dad was right in what he believed. When she was a college student in America she was invited to a church. Even though she went for social reasons it was there she heard about Jesus Christ and chose to follow Him. Her life is now full of joy and blessings. Later both of her parents became believers in Jesus. Most of us in our group shared with him our source of joy. We gave him a Bible and one to the lady who owned the school.

Our day to walk a portion of the Great Wall of China ended at the border with North Korea. They were amazed at this 75-year-old climbing the steep steps. How good God is to me allowing me to participate. After our walk on the Wall, we returned to Feng Cheng to have lunch. Some ate at KFC and others at a Korean restaurant. Afterwards we all had our feet massaged.

*The level of your understanding of the Gospel
determines the level of your abiding.*

My first Christmas in Thailand was incredibly special, made so by fellow co-workers who had homes they graciously opened for us singles to celebrate with them. What great cooks they were as well.

New Year's Day 2005 found me in Rayong, Thailand staying in a Penthouse on the coast overlooking the Gulf of Thailand with my friend and her family. We spent hours in the study of God's Word as well as enjoying the sea.

At the end of January our team packed our office and moved to Pattaya to work at my first AGM (Annual General Meeting) and stayed there until February 17th. I was blessed beyond measure meeting the people with whom I had been corresponding since June 2004. Rejoiced with those with whom I had visited in China in October 2004 at the manifold grace of God and hearing again their joy in serving our Lord. It was an incredibly special time together to meet face to face with those whom you had been corresponding with via email only.

In March, the ladies began a Beth Moore Bible Study, "Believing God" which I recommend to everyone. It has a powerful message for both women and men.

In April, our team went by overnight train to Bangkok where we caught a flight to the island of Phuket, one of the places the tsunami hit. We saw the rebuilding four months after the tsunami and met two of our workers there and heard of the relief efforts firsthand. Later my son-in-law Dr. John Gibson participated in getting an injured volunteer flown out of Phuket to Bangkok for medical treatment as he was able to communicate in Thai with the doctors there.

On May 22nd, I awoke to a flood in my Chiang Mai apartment on the 16th floor. Certainly, a rude awakening. I was due to depart in an hour and a half for Mongolia. By God's grace I didn't panic, but it was difficult getting dressed in a flood and wading out into the hall also flooding to get to the first floor for help. A Thai security guard came back with me and found the shut off valve out in the hall for my apartment. The hose by the toilet came apart while I was sleeping, and a fountain of water erupted for hours while I slept. A man from our office came, took over the problem and helped me wade out with luggage to catch my ride to the airport.

*It only takes a little faith to move a mountain.*

I flew first to Bangkok where I would catch a flight to Seoul, Korea. After eleven hours in the Seoul airport awaiting my flight with three team members from Georgia who joined me there. We flew the same flight into Mongolia. What a blessing this journey became with my people group and the Georgia team. The men from Georgia are recovering alcoholics, but mighty in God's spirit since being freed from their addiction. The men met with separate groups of alcoholics in Mongolia giving their testimony of God's sufficient grace to set them free. Many found faith in Christ through their witness. One of the men was a strength exhibitionist who in America speaks to youth groups about the strength of the Lord. I witnessed his physical strength exhibition along with the others. No other man present could do what he was able to do.

I stayed with Mary I had met 10 years before in North Carolina never dreaming that someday I would be spending 12 days with her in Mongolia. My joyous host taught me so much about giving thanks in all things. Even when you have no electricity or water for hours, which occurs frequently, her grateful joy remains steadfast. Her assignment for me was to share my testimony with a Mongolian grandmother 35 miles out in the Gobi Dessert. The grandmother's daughter had become a Christian a few weeks earlier and she wanted no part of it. They hoped that a grandmother talking with a grandmother might have influence.

Eleven of us went in a hired van into the desert. When we

arrived at the gher, the grandmother had been preparing a meal for her visitors. Since I was the eldest person present, I was offered the first drink of hot mare's milk with additives (not sure what). My stomach had not fully recovered from the hamburger I ate in the Bangkok airport on my way to Mongolia. As I looked down at the hot drink, my sunglasses fell off my face into the drink. Thankfully, the drink was taken and spooned outside to some spirits. I wasn't offered a second chance, and I didn't want one. My stomach was so unsettled I didn't want to put anything into it.

After visiting we went outside to see her livestock of camels, sheep and goats. Before returning inside, my interpreter arranged three exceptionally low stools for the grandmother, me and herself beside the gher. I gave my testimony in English and Duma interpreted it into Mongolian. Then the grandmother had something to say to me, "The Mongolian government was erecting a statue in honor of her father for his ministry to the Mongolian people as a Dali Lama Buddhist priest that summer." Then I told her how my God had healed me of cancer which struck her in a powerful way because in her mind if you got cancer you would die, with no hope of healing. After that she kept curiously watching me until we all departed.

Ten days later the grandmother was in town for a school celebration for the children provided by the government. She had several grandchildren in town. She also sent word that she would like to meet with me again. When we did meet, about an hour before our team's scheduled departure. I shared with her Scriptures that were read to her from the Mongolian Bible. After a lengthy time of reading the pastor's wife asked her if she wanted to receive Jesus Christ into her life and she responded positively. It was a long prayer led by the pastor's wife. When they finished praying, I was informed that she had accepted the Lord. I looked at her and said we are now sisters in God's family. She hugged me and kept alternating between kissing me on both of my cheeks. She clung to me and would have gone home with me if it were possible.

Later, when my friend Mary would visit with her, the grandmother would point to our picture together and say, "My Lila."

A year later the grandmother was stricken with liver cancer. She lasted six months. Around her deathbed were her children, sisters and church members. She raised her hands and said, "Hallelu...." Not getting the last syllable out before she entered the presence of her Lord. Her funeral was the first Christian funeral ever held in that city.

I returned from Mongolia the night of June 10th only 40 hours before our team left for China. We went through Hong Kong for the second time without ever seeing the skyline. I bought postcards showing the city in all its splendor. At our destination in China, we enjoyed spiritual refreshment together with other believers strengthening us for future service.

*If God the Father is sovereign everywhere, you can rest anywhere.*

I began teaching ESL (English as a Second Language) on the weekends with Chinese in Thailand. It was a special blessing which I enjoyed teaching for weeks. The owners of the place where the Chinese congregation met for worship and where I taught did not like the Christian meetings. They are searching for another place to meet.

September 18th a co-worker and I flew into China where we went to several cities encouraging our people on the field. In one city we were included in an English class in a Minority Middle School where the teacher set up three corners in the classroom for English conversation. I had one of the corners to engage the students to practice their English-speaking skills. One in the group asked me where my ancestors had come from. Your ancestors are important in China.

In one city we heard about our workers going with volunteers from America up a mountain to a Buddhist temple. A woman with her 14-year-old mute daughter was entreating her god at the temple for the healing of her daughter. When the woman was leaving, she noticed the Americans and asked if their God could heal her daughter. She had gone daily for years to the temple pleading for her daughter's healing to no avail. The Americans shared with her that she needed to believe in the Creator God before He would heal her daughter. After explaining the way of salvation, the woman gladly prayed to receive Jesus Christ as her Savior. Then she asked if God would then heal her daughter. They responded that if she asked God herself in faith believing then He would heal. The woman prayed to the Creator God asking Him to heal her daughter. Afterwards the group started walking down the mountain. The mute girl ran past them and turned looking upward at them raised her arms and said, "Jesus loves me." Her first words ever spoken.

I then traveled to Tibet with a co-worker. We took altitude medicine before the trip to prepare our bodies for the high altitude. We visited several cities before flying into Lhasa. In Lhasa we learned about the history and the different Tibetan people groups. Some Tibetans had told them that they had seen Jesus in the sky. One group of Tibetans told how Jesus had spoken to them through a TV that wasn't even plugged in. We grieved over the spiritual blindness as we witnessed people falling prostrate repeatedly before sacred (to them) buildings and places and burning incense, but no joy on their faces. On our last day we planned to tour the Potola Palace. Our ride in a rickshaw was perilous and only by the protection of God am I still alive to tell. With so many pilgrims at the Palace we were told to come back in the afternoon, but we had other plans. We went to the summer palace instead. We ate yak burgers (which were good) and were carefully guided through the bazaar. The remarkable stories we heard, and experiences were memorable. I am glad I have pictures to revisit these precious memories. I even danced with the Tibetans. While we were on this trip it flooded in Chiang Mai and the flood waters came into our office building on the first floor a few feet deep. What a clean-up lay before us.

Right after that trip we traveled into southern China with our team through Hong Kong and Macau. These trips bonded us into a family which lessened our loss being away from our biological families.

Always, Thanksgiving, Christmas and the New Year were special "family gatherings" again lessening the loss of being absent from our families back in the States.

*You can't disappoint God.*

2006 was to be especially remembered because I got to go where I had wanted to go for 60 years – ALASKA!!! Colorado had always been my favorite state since I first went there in 1967, but after Alaska, it got bumped to second place. However, the special part of this trip is that it was shared with both of my daughters and their spouses, plus my two youngest granddaughters, nephew Jeff and his family (wife Lisa and son Joshua, 19 and daughter Anna, 22). Both couples were celebrating 25 years of marriage, and I was completing my visits to all 50 States. After not seeing family for many months this was icing on the cake.

In Denali National Park we saw eight grizzly bears, elk, moose, foxes, caribou, sheep and the state bird, Willow ptarmigan. And the most magnificent scene of all: Mount McKinley, now known as Denali, from just 35 miles away. We were at the closet point to that mountain on a road. When climbers want to scale the mountain, they must fly into base camp. It looked like a stairway to heaven. The bus driver said that we must have good karma. I wished I were close enough to the front to tell her no, isn't karma, but answered prayer to the One who created this magnificent planet. The driver went on to say that only about 25% of visitors to Alaska ever get to see Denali as it is usually shrouded in clouds. And we saw it from every location that it could be seen in all its beauty. One of my dreams of a lifetime had now been fulfilled.

*Disappointment is an unmet expectation.*

Back in Georgia I met my first great-granddaughter, Danielle Jewel Echols born the previous December while I was still in Thailand. I did talk with Gracie, the proud mom, right after she had delivered Jewel. I am so thrilled that she has beautiful big brown eyes like her mother, Gracie. Her brother Nathan then passed his seventh birthday and was happy to have a sister. Nathan had expressed a desire to have a sister and not a brother so he would not have to share his toys. My daughter Sue is thrilled to have a granddaughter after four grandsons. She is a grandmother to her stepdaughter Vicky's two sons, Collin and Jack, as well as Nathan and Jonathan.

---

*What God initiates (source), He will sustain
(supply), and He will fulfill (goal).*

I lived in College Station, Texas with my daughter Linda and her family as we had spent years apart while they lived in Thailand. I got involved in the Discovery program at the church which had different classes offered to internationals. We had more than 50 different countries represented among the attendees. Linda and I taught basic English to women from different countries. Those who already knew English had other classes to choose from such as, cooking, gardening, crocheting, knitting, sewing garments and scrapbooking. It was a blessing as some came to faith in Christ during those meetings. In the general assembly before going to class, each Wednesday a different country presented a power point or the equivalent about their home country. They would also provide food native to their countries for the group.

On Monday evenings I would go to the Lighthouse Mission where we had Bible study with former lady prisoners. It was beautiful to watch those who had come to faith transform observing their sadness turn to joy.

On Tuesday mornings I volunteered at the Hope Pregnancy Center where we counseled women coming for a pregnancy test and a free sonogram. I had the joy of leading a few of the ladies to faith in Christ. It was great fun when a couple earned "Mommie dollars" by attending classes then got to spend those "dollars" in Hannah's closet. The Center emails keep me in the loop with all the ministry that continues there. These are wonderful co-workers who love the Lord with all their hearts.

*Preach God's light to your darkness.*

When asked to return to Thailand, I had to go through all the physicals again to determine if I were still cancer free. Thankfully, none was found, and I was medically cleared to return.

On April 24, 2008, I was back in Thailand for another two-year term. It is wonderful serving again with my former co-workers and meeting others who had arrived after my first term. We have a talented team working with a loyal Thai staff (same staff as before). They are very dear to me.

This December our team participates in providing gifts for children and their teachers in a mountain village. Also, as a team we are providing Christmas gifts for Tribal children living in the Hostel next to our office and for the Korean orphanage nearby.

Our church group in Chiang Mai is reaching out to people in neighborhoods by fishing:

**F** — Finding interested people.

**I** — Inviting people into our homes for refreshments.

**S** — Sharing our testimony when following up.

**H** — Helping them grow as a Christian.

All this began with prayer-walking throughout the neighborhoods.

Three weeks after my arrival I went with the Thai staff high in the mountains to attend our guard's wedding on May 17th in his home Karen village. Quite different from any other wedding that I had ever attended but was so blessed by the smile on the face of the groom when I showed up. I was able to share my witness of Christ with the attendees as Jiab translated for me. I was the only foreigner in the village. I have a lovely picture of me next to the groom with his beautiful bride on his other side along with the Thai staff. I did substantial praying up and then back down the mountain on treacherous muddy roads. God mercifully took us to and from the village safely.

The following week I became quite ill and remained sick for about four weeks with only five days of wellness between two separate problems. During this time, I lost 16 pounds of weight which I have not been able to regain in Thailand. It is difficult for me to find a variety of foods that my body can digest. I frequently eat the same old menu that is agreeable.

In October I went to China for eleven days and had the privilege of traveling to where Lottie Moon served for nearly forty years. I have a picture of me standing by a monument to her which had been buried and hidden during the Cultural Revolution. Also, a picture of me with the pastor and the caretakers of the ongoing church where Lottie taught. Volunteers from Georgia built a larger church next door to accommodate the regular weekly attendees of around 700. The balcony will accommodate space for a total church capacity of 1300 which is filled during Christmas and Easter services. Wulin Shenghui Church of Penglai in Shandong Provine has been designated as a nationally recognized historic and cultural site by the Chinese government.

During this trip I was involved with students in two Universities in English classes interacting in the classrooms with the students. "Office" hours were also held four evenings a week for students seeking to know about our God, studying the Bible or conversational English. We had crowds of students for all those varied reasons, meeting in separate rooms during "Office" hours. I had the privilege of sharing my testimony of God's love and mercy to me with groups in each room. By appointment I met with several girl students on campus. The students were curious about a near 80-year-old traveling by herself. Well, I never travel alone, as the Lord is always with me. Those students now correspond with me via email, so I have an ongoing opportunity to mentor them. It was such a wonderful week I didn't want to return to Thailand.

Again, wonderful holidays of Thanksgiving, Christmas and New Year's Day with "family" here in Thailand. In January we packed up our office and headed back to AGM meetings. Again, we were with hundreds of like-minded people from all over East Asia region.

March 25, 2009, Migdalia and Jeremiah presented a new son Jonah William Schultz my third great-grandson. His big brother Jonathan had asked the Lord for a brother and God answered his tender prayers. Looking forward to holding him soon.

*The view only gets better the closer you are to God.*

Saturday, April 4th, I celebrated my 80th birthday in Thailand with my co-workers and our Thai staff. A Christian Thai lady talked about her coming to faith in Christ after having been a Buddhist. She and her husband own three language schools and are an enormous influence on those they encounter.

My new Filipino friend Charlotte sang at the party. She has a great solo voice. Several weeks ago, at the church gathering, she sang my all-time favorite song "The Holy City" which was thrilling to hear again. My paternal grandmother's name was Charlotte Adele, so we hit it off good from the start.

My friend Gary Harthcock wrote a poem about me and had it framed. He read to the group what he had written.

## TO LILA COX
## ON HER EIGHTEITH BIRTHDAY
### APRIL 4, 2009

Though eighty now, she does not fit the mold;
Nor does she shuffle, but her steps are bold.
Some other signs are missing just as well,
She labors long but does not "sit a spell."
She drives her tiny car through thick and thin,
As if the race ahead she now must win.
But calmness shows an inner peace is there
That helps her smile, and love and always care.
Her children are a source of joy to her
And she is just the mother they prefer.
We ask ourselves how did this come to be?
What can we learn from this, both you and me?
Ask Lila, and she'll quickly speak with grace,
"It comes from God for those who seek His face."

Gary Harthcock
Chiang Mai, Thailand
April 4, 2009

Gary will soon be 90, and his wife Evelyn will be 89 in October. He spoke about their ministry over the years with Buddhist monks teaching them English in their monasteries. They authored many books and freely gave to those teaching internationals the English language. They have served on four continents and continue to serve in Thailand. Gary's quote "I'll retire when the devil retires" written and taped to his desk, which he reads every day. I too resemble that quote about retiring.

I introduced my friends who have a foundation for supporting hilltribe orphans by providing Christian families with help to take orphans to raise in their home with their own children rather than build orphanage buildings.

After the party, Charlotte, her sister and I went to Im Jai orphanage and picked up Dong, whom I have known for several years. Linda wanted to adopt him many years ago, but it didn't work out. He is eleven days younger than our Kaitlyn and has been in the orphanage since age five. He really liked Charlotte and she plans to get him from time to time and take him to her home so he can have some family.

This year I said farewell to my two brothers Marvin on March 6 before I arrived in Florida for my birthday, and Bobby on October 18 after I had returned to Thailand. Rex's only full brother Bob Cox died as well.

April 8, 2009, at 1:40 a.m. I am scheduled to fly by Korean Air to Incheon (airport serving Seoul). Change planes in Incheon for a direct flight to Atlanta, Georgia. Scheduled to land in Atlanta at 10:30 a.m. on April 8th, then on to Florida for my 80th birthday party with family and friends.

Oh, what a party we had! My girls performed a skit portraying Nellie and me living together in Sateke Village. I asked Kolja if that was what it was really like living with us two old ladies. He said, "Pretty much." We all had a good laugh. Katie played "As the Deer Pants for the Water" on her flute, a favorite of mine. I had stated beforehand that this celebration would be a dress rehearsal for my funeral and Katie informed me that if I said it one more time she would not participate. Many friends and family stayed the weekend with us at Lake Yale in Florida celebrating. They said such wonderful things about me and expressed dear and cherished memories.

*"Do not cast me off in the time of my old age;*
*forsake me not when my strength is spent.*
*So even to old age and gray hairs, O God, do not*
*forsake me, until I proclaim your might to another*
*generation, your power to all those to come."*

Psalm 71:9, 18

# OLD AGE AND GOING STRONG

## 2010 – 2019

Upon my return from Thailand to America on March 20, 2010, I was soon involved in our church's Mission Conference. I helped Sue with the Poland display and hosting my sister-in-law Vivian and her friend Mary who came from Florida to experience First Baptist Church of Woodstock's missions conference. Ludie and Barbara Creech, with their three children, are serving in Ireland with OM (Operation Mobilization). When they were presenting their work and requests for involvement I was asked if I would consider working in Ireland for six months enabling a co-worker to take a six-month furlough. This Irish man, with his wife and family, have been serving there for 12 years with no furlough.

OM has several ways of outreach to meet the needs of the people. In Ireland they have the Big Red Bus which travels to communities with children's holiday clubs, youth programs and family events. Also, a youth conference called "Connect" is attended by hundreds of Irish youths. OM Ships travel around the world with medical doctors and dentists, while docked people are invited aboard for treatment and to have needs met. Impact Ireland, their short-term summer program, attracts volunteers from all over the world to work alongside local churches, schools and conduct sporting events around the country. My German exchange student Kolja served in Ireland with a group from the USA his first summer back home in Germany in 2002.

My assignment would be to do the financial work in the office for the worker requesting his first furlough. In addition to that, I would be involved with churches alongside Ludie and Barbara Creech as they serve. An additional bonus would be the "on location" grandmother for the Creech's three children. However, God had another person in mind who was a better fit, I was no longer needed.

Easter Sunday our family celebrated my 81st birthday and worshiped at CrossView Community Church where Gracie's husband Danny is the lead pastor.

Sue's first short story "Triumphant Transitions" was published in the Christian Authors Guild's anthology America Remembered in May. Also in May, Sue and I flew to Texas for Katie's graduation from high school after Sue's PRK eye surgery the day before to correct her vision from cataract surgery done last year.

*Surrender all my desires to you ~ keeping first things first.*

From July 18th until September 20th, I lived in pain, but He has set me free. Praise His glorious Name! September 20, 2010, I slept only 45 minutes. After a time of trying to adjust my body again I had only another 45-minute sleep. Nothing was giving me real relief in my legs and feet so I could sleep.

After watching a sermon by Pastor Johnny Hunt, I knelt at the foot of the bed that night and submitted my body to the Lord Jesus Christ to be His body - not mine. I told the Lord since it was His body and not mine, I would accept whatever He chose to do with it. I knew that nothing is impossible with God, but also know that His ways are not my ways. Prayed that whatever would bring Him the greatest glory would take place in His body occupied by me as my earthly housing.

After submitting my body to the Lord to be His and not mine

I was able to sleep for hours. Awakened at 8 a.m. the morning of September 21st with absolutely no pain - anywhere in my body. Also, my spine felt straight from scoliosis. My daughter Linda examined my spine, and it looked straight to her. Then Linda and I measured my height next to hers and found I was tall again. God's miracle of healing has taken place in His body for His glory.

My prayer is that I will remain conscious of the fact that I am residing in the Lord's body, not mine, thereby yielding to His Lordship over me and listening to what He wants me to do for His glory in ministering to others in His name. What an awesome God we serve!

Michael and Sue traveled to Burleson, Texas for Thanksgiving with the Gibsons and me. They spent most of the week laying tile in the Gibson's home in College Station with hopes that it would sell. Fred and Joan Orcutt came over on Friday of that week. We met the Orcutts at First Baptist Church of Woodstock years ago. It is always good to catch up with friends.

The first major event of 2012 was my son-in-law Michael's hip replacement surgery in early February. That has not gone well and continues to plague him.

*God has already prepared the way; He's just preparing you.*

Daughter Sue is teaching the Lydia Class at church each Sunday, working full time at a law firm in Atlanta, President of Christian Authors Guild, plus other involvements. She enjoys being the grandmother to Jeremiah's two sons, Jonathan and Jonah plus the four in Gracie and Danny Echols' home: Daniel, Nathan, Jewel and Brianna. And when Michael and Sue get to Illinois, they enjoy visiting with Michael's daughter Vicky, her husband and children Collin, Jack and Sarina.

Kimberly Gibson graduated from Baylor University in May with a degree in English and specialization in Linguistics. She hopes to become a professor of English/Linguistics. Presently she is working on a master's degree in Linguistics at North Texas University. She also teaches a class there as well as tutoring students.

Kaitlyn Gibson spent the summer on the mission field in Honduras. She is in her third year at the University of Missouri in the school of nursing. She already has a missionary heart.

All four Gibsons (John, Linda, Kim and Katie) are in Thailand involved. John is replacing Dr. Doug Derbyshire as the treating physician in the Bangkla Baptist Clinic to keep the clinic open while Dr. Doug is in the States. Linda and the girls are participating in outreach community events.

Daughter Linda still works as a nurse anesthetist, teaching nursing classes online with Liberty University and involved with refugees in Fort Worth, Texas. Her husband John is director of Global Medicine at John Peter Smith Hospital in Fort Worth.

2013 finds me still traversing between daughters. Sue in Georgia and Linda in Texas each providing a home for me. I spend time with one or the other and their families according to family events. Both places keep me incredibly involved with great Biblical teaching, great preaching, wonderful friendships and a loving family with whom I share life.

The biggest news in our family this year is the engagement of Kaitlyn Diane Gibson, my youngest granddaughter, to Caleb Huhmann. They met at the campus church at the University of Missouri. From that church they have been on three mission trips, one in the States and two separate trips to Honduras.

*God loves me best. God loves you best. Because*
*God loves all His children best.*

On May 24, 2014, escorted by her father John Gibson, Kaitlyn walked down a grassy aisle on a farm in Central Missouri to the Christian song, "10,000 Reasons" to stand beside her beloved. Caleb wore a radiant smile as they invited the parents from each side, plus me, to join a sand-pouring ceremony symbolizing the intertwining of spiritual influence we each had in their lives to this point. The soloist sang "Oceans" beautifully and I prayed:

"Our Father, we commend Caleb and Katie to You for Your blessing. May they come to know Your Word more fully and thereby know You more deeply. May they show their love to You through obedience to whatever You call them to do. May Your pursuit of them captivate their hearts like never before.

May they, as husband and wife, follow wherever You lead them to make You better known. Grant them a clear vision of Your purpose, and Your Love for them be expressed in their love for each other, a faithful love, a serving love.

May the legacy they leave point to Your Faithfulness and unconditional Love for future generations to be encouraged to follow You.

In Jesus Christ's Name, I pray. Amen"

Also, in May Katie graduates with a degree in Nursing and Caleb with a master's degree in accounting. Katie plans to continue her education toward a Doctorate in Nursing. Caleb plans to become a Certified Public Accountant (CPA). They will make their home in Kansas City, Missouri where Caleb has been interning with an accounting firm that will employ him full time after graduation.

Kimberly Gibson will complete her master's degree in Linguistics at the University of North Texas. She lives about an hour's drive north of her parents' home, making it more convenient to come home for visits than her sister because she is much nearer.

The total of my descendants are two daughters, four grandchildren, and six great-grandchildren at this moment.

*There is a sweet contentment that comes from*
*living in a perpetual state of need and fulfillment*
*from God's provision. – Mike Donehey*

August 30th, I flew with three teammates (daughter Sue, Patti Cornelius and Maggie Hanson) from the Atlanta airport, to Charlotte, North Carolina, to Munich, Germany, to Poland on a mission trip. In Poland we partnered with Pat Weathersbee, our church's Send International missionary. She had arranged for us to minister to ladies and their children at a shelter in Ścinawa for three days. Each day one of would tell a dramatized story of a woman in the Bible as well as play games with prizes, have activities and crafts for the children, and teach the ladies how to make spiral scarves with the knitting needles and yarn provided them. Most of the ladies completed two scarves each. Our Polish interpreter told her personal story how her life was changed from being an atheist to becoming a Christian, wife of a minister and mother of a daughter and a son. Her life story resonated with the women in the shelter. Maggie's young granddaughter raised money and supplies to give each child a bag of school supplies. The ladies and their children were overwhelmed with the bounty given. Their lives were impacted by the love shown to them.

Next, we arrived at a center for handicapped people of different ages. Together they made decorations for the upcoming Women's Conference to be held in their facility. Each person received a personal craft item which they could make and keep. The following day the ladies from Lubin Baptist Church lead the teaching sessions for the Women's Conference while our team provided and served lunch for the attendees. The ladies had a fun time while names were drawn for door prizes. Several ladies from Ścinawa attended the Conference. I was the Friday night speaker sharing two out of numerous episodes in my life that I have lived the Bible verse, Isaiah 65:24, "Before they call, I will answer, and while they are yet speaking, I will hear."

One afternoon we participated in an English Conversation Corner and another time visited Ella in her specialty coffee shop. Ella, the coffee shop owner, came and served coffee to the ladies at the Conference.

From Poland we flew via Copenhagen to Dublin, capital of

Ireland. Our missionaries, the Creeches with Operation Mobilization arranged our brief visit with OM workers and the Emersion International Team from four countries. We toured Lacken House, headquarters for OM Ireland, meeting the staff, sharing with them and them with us, how our Father is working. Spent an evening of fellowship with a group from the Ballinasloe Church. What a precious time with God's family hearing how they minister to the people in Ireland. Sue and I visited a Muslim lady in Roscommon who had requested we come to her home. She has a young son in kindergarten and is pregnant with her second child. She asked various questions about Christ. And in prayer we asked the Lord to bless her.

Serving with Barbara and Ludie Creech, whom we personally support through OM (Operation Mobilization) are dearly beloved friends. Sue and Barbara worked together at FBC Woodstock before God called them to Ireland. Their youngest daughter is my namesake Lila Katherine Creech. I am truly blessed to be so honored.

On November 23rd I fell and broke my left wrist, but thankfully healing is taking place; however, I am still wearing an ACE brace. The Lord has been teaching me much through this. Unfortunately, I have had to give up knitting because knitting is relaxing therapy for me. I'm grateful I was able to knit layette outfits for all my great grandchildren beforehand.

*Circumstances in life will test your character.*

A Lifeway bookstore near Linda's home in Ft. Worth, Texas, hosted a book signing by Charles Stanley. We were amazed by the crowded lines weaving among the aisles of books, waiting patiently to meet Dr. Charles Stanley. Linda and I have read several of his books and I bought two for an autograph by the author. Our neighborhood friend, and nurse, Monica Cameron came with us, and we chatted about how the spiritual influence of Dr. Stanley's writings had deepened our own walk with the Savior. When my turn came, Dr. Stanley greeted me and asked me some questions, then signed his name with care. It interested me that as many African American neighbors like Monica were just as eager to meet him as were we, showing the breadth of his influence.

*The people I would regard as having great Christian character are invariably people who have learned how to handle life in the crucible. – Chuck Swindoll*

Early in December 2016 Sue and I traveled to Ecuador to visit longtime missionary friends, Olgar and Mary Jaramillo, serving in Macas, Ecuador. I had known Mary in Bloomington, Indiana long before she left for Ecuador and married Olgar. Sue said this was the most relaxing vacation ever as we took siestas every afternoon. Mary, a wonderful cook and tour guide, showed us incredible hospitality. I was given the privilege of sharing my testimony in the church one evening. During our visit, their daughter Ivana was trying to decide where to go to college in the States for an EMT/ paramedic's degree. They were looking at a school in North Carolina when Sue asked, "who does she known in North Carolina?" Mary replied, "no one." Sue suggested they check on a technical college less than five miles from her home in Georgia to see if the degree was offered there. It was and later they decided that would be the school for Ivana, Chattahoochee Tech. Ivana moved into Michael and Sue's home in August to begin her training as an EMT / paramedic.

*Everything we do matters to God and is used by Him.*

Easter 2017 in Ocala, Florida, was a special blessing as several cousins joined Sue, Michael, Linda and I to worship together at First Baptist Church of Ocala. Memorable were the triumphant hymns sung accompanied by an orchestra. The flautist praised our Risen Lord in expressive sign language all during the worship time. My good and long-time friend Elaine Frameli sat with our family, and we all ate together afterwards. I have been Elaine's spiritual mom and mentor for decades.

On April 21, 2018, my great grandson, Nathan Michael Echols, married Lindsey. I was asked to pray a blessing over their marriage right before they were pronounced Mr. and Mrs.

When I was back in Georgia, Sue and Linda drove me to visit my friend and co-laborer in missions Maggie Hanson only a couple of weeks before she died. Her daughters were doing their best to make her final days cheerful, but admitted to us that they were trying liquid THC to help with her pain and nausea from pancreatic cancer and thought they had overdosed her that day. Maggie was able to chat a bit but was obviously drowsy. We prayed for her and said our last goodbyes. Our beloved Maggie died on May 25, 2018.

Near the end of June, I flew to Texas to see my friends the Loyd family in Bryan, Texas, a week before they were to return to Thailand. Ryan Lloyd, who is a medical doctor, was to teach in the Thai medical school. His wife Janseng Loyd is Thai. They met at the clinic my daughter Linda and her husband Dr. John began in Nan, Thailand. Janseng was the lab technician and spoke fair English. Now she keeps busy caring for their six children.

Connected again with friends all over Texas and worshiped with them. Enjoyed mentoring a young Chinese lady Qinyan Li at Linda's house in Ft. Worth. She and I had numerous extended prayer sessions together and I watched her grow significantly in our Lord. Qinyan Li will always be Sophia to me as I cannot pronounce her Chinese name. This also opened the door to mentor her friend. Her friend's husband was a businessman in China when he met his wife. Later they lived in Ft. Worth. He was treated this past year for lung cancer. I met him two days before I returned to Georgia. We had two things in common: cancer and China. Therefore, we shared stories of those experiences. He showed me a chart he had on evolution and asked me to explain it to him. I offered the reasons I didn't believe in evolution. Our time together ended because of the hour; therefore, after I returned to Georgia, I mailed information on that subject to him.

Ivana Jaramillo and Nick Dietz married on November 24, 2018, in Bloomington, Indiana. I didn't attend the wedding, but Michael,

Sue and Jonah did. Nick came to live with Ivana and us at Sue's house in January 2019.

The whole Moore Clan was present to bid farewell to my sister-in-law Georgia as her son Rev. Jeffery Clayton Moore presided over her funeral. Jeff's sisters hosted the meal afterwards. During that time, we were amazed by stories of how Georgia sang praise songs with a few ladies visiting from her Lutheran church up until just minutes before she slipped into eternity with her Lord and Savior Jesus Christ! Aging has a way of impacting our thoughts of the end (or is it the end?). My sister Thelma Adele concluded her stay here on earth two Decembers ago (12-8-2016) and my sister-in-law Georgia Howie Moore passed from this life December 6, 2018. For each of these dear ones and myself, death is not the end, but a new beginning of life in the glorious presence of Jesus.

*Help me trust Your goodness and love for me.*

As planned on April 4, 2019, my 90th birthday celebration began with meeting Ching at the Billy Graham Library along with Drs. Rich and Susan Bae who also served in China. Rich serenaded me with some songs as we ate together in the library's small restaurant. Returning to Sue's house for a 3-day open house April 5 through 7 – I let Sue know that if she got tired, she could take a nap as people were coming to see me. I greeted guests each day and had wonderful visits with family and friends coming from all over. I received over 60 cards brought by guests and some by mail who couldn't make the trip. Plus, about $200 in gift cards to purchase the books I still want to read!

The Mission Possible Sunday School class, which I attend when I am residing with Sue, traveled to Newnan, Georgia to celebrate the marriage of Bill and Shirley Baker, both widowed and strong Christians. It was a lovely, God honoring wedding.

Kaitlyn Humann received her doctorate as a Nurse Practitioner in Kansas City, Missouri on May 19, 2019. My nephew Jeff and wife Lisa met us for the big celebration along with Bruce and MaryBeth

Huhmann, Caleb's parents. She and her husband Caleb are big NFL Kansas City Chiefs fans.

In June, my daughter Linda had major ear/brain surgery and I was helping her as she recuperated at their golf course home in Burleson, Texas. She returned to her anesthesia practice in July after a quick trip to Mt. Rushmore with John and their children for the 4th of July holiday.

On September 2, 2019, Kimberly Gibson and Khiem Tran got engaged. Khiem told Kimberly you're more Asian than I am as Kimberly grew up in Thailand and Khiem, although full blooded Vietnamese, has never been to Vietnam.

Katie and Caleb left for their first mission term with the IMB in Bangkla, Thailand. They have committed as career missionaries like Linda and John. I'm glad to live long enough to witness subsequent generations serving in missions. Gracie took Jewel on her first short term mission trip at age 13 to serve with Sue in Poland. Sue has been going to Poland since 2007. Neat that four generations (me, Sue, Gracie and Jewel) have served the people of Poland. Nathan traveled to Africa for his first overseas mission trip as well as his dad on separate trips. I pray that my love and legacy of missions continues for God's glory.

Mary Jaramillo arrived in October from Ecuador with Ivana's help as Mary was coming home to Sue's house for her remaining days. Mary stated, "My life fits into three suitcases." Sad reflection of her life as a missionary in Ecuador. One of the suitcases contained her China dishes which we used for our Thanksgiving dinner. What a privilege to care for a missionary friend in her dying days.

Sue, Michael, their children and grandchildren went to North Carolina on December 28th to celebrate Christmas and Jonathan's 18th birthday. Instead of giving gifts they like to do something together as a family for their Christmas celebration. With their son-in-law Danny serving as a Pastor getting away on Christmas is unlikely. This trip to North Carolina was for snow tubing. They had planned to spend the night and return home the next day. Sue called after their tubing adventure to check on us (me, Mary and

Ivana). Mary had just died, and Ivana was wailing in grief. I gave the phone to Ivana so Sue could speak to her. Michael and Sue headed home at once and arrived before they had taken Mary's body to the funeral home.

> *"Lord, make me to know my end and (to appreciate) the measure of my days – what it is: let me know and realize how frail I am (how transient is my stay here). Behold, you have made my days as (short as) handbreadths, and my lifetime is as nothing in Your sight. Truly every man at his best is merely a breath!"*
>
> *Psalm 39:4-5 AMP*

# THE BEGINNING OF THE END

## 2020 – February 16, 2023

2020 began as a sad affair for us as we mourned the passing of our dear and long-time friend Mary Jaramillo. Her son Josiah came from Ecuador to be with Ivana and together they spread her ashes at Lake Allatoona. Then Josiah took the rest of Mary's ashes back to Ecuador and with the company of family and friends spread the remainder of her ashes in the river that runs through Macas, Mary's hometown for many years.

On March 29, 2020, Kimberly and Khiem Tran were married in Dallas, Texas at the same church her parents had married, and I had a stroke that evening at Sue's house. I don't remember anything, but Sue tells me about my ordeal.

She recounts that we were cooking dinner and baking cookies with both of us in the kitchen when I told her I thought I was going to pass out. Sue came over to me and asked if I had drunk enough water that day and I replied yes but fell into her arms out cold.

Because of COVID-19 I was not taken to the hospital. Sue called Linda and asked her what to do. Linda told her all the things to assess me, rub my feet, rub my sternum, check my eyes' reaction to a light ~ nothing ~ I was non-responsive to any stimuli. As I lay on the couch (Michael had helped Sue move me there), the family gathered. Gracie and her family and Ivana and Nick; Jeremiah was on the road traveling with his job. Ivana, studying in paramedics tried all the same tests Linda suggested and still no response. Songs were sung, prayers prayed, thinking I was on my way to heaven. Around 1 a.m. I began to respond by squeezing Ivana's hand, then talking. I even talked to Jeremiah by phone. Everyone went home and I went to bed upstairs closer to Sue and not in my bedroom downstairs so she could tend to me.

Linda flew in from Texas and the girls took me to the doctors to confirm my stroke and then to cardiologist for my atrial fibrillation. I began taking Eliquis to help prevent another stroke.

I had my birthday via Skype from Sue's home with everyone calling in through Skype to wish me a happy 92nd birthday. I do not remember talking to my family, but everyone told me I looked good. My biggest problem besides my memory was double vision. Sue advised me to close one eye to see without the double vision as she had experienced double vision after her retinal detachment surgery. We asked everyone to pray that I would be able to see without the double vision as I love to read and am a regular Bible reader. God again was gracious to me, and my double vision cleared up and I was able to read again.

Linda came to take me back to her home in Burleson, Texas where I enjoy having friends come, visit and play games. Linda had me doing math and puzzles to help my brain recover after the stroke. I can still win at Rummikub even after my stroke. It's all about the numbers.

December 7, 2020, Daniel, Nathan, and Noah Echols were in a tragic accident on I-285, the bypass around Atlanta. Daniel was thrown from the truck and died. Nathan and Noah were treated and released to go home. I was in Texas at Linda's home, but Linda flew to Georgia to be present at Daniel's funeral which was held at West Ridge Church in Dallas, Georgia. Gracie did not want the memory of Daniel's casket in the worship center of their church. It would be too difficult to worship with that visual burned into their memories.

COVID-19 came to Linda's home. John worked at the hospital and brought COVID-19 home. During my COVID bout I had breathing problems and Hospice brought oxygen and a nebulizer to help me. I have recovered and only used a rescue inhaler.

I arrived in Georgia on December 31st (New Year's Eve) and getting settled in. After having COVID-19 in Texas with Linda and John and continuing Hospice care here at Sue's house, I'm not reading emails often and try to rest periodically throughout the day. I enjoy hearing from others via text, phone calls or cards that I read and cherish.

March 30, 3021 my great-great-granddaughter Isabelle Rose Echols was born to Nathan and Lindsay. The following Sunday, April 4, 2021, Easter and my birthday, I got to hold Izzy for the first time at five days old.

The swallow test taken in Texas indicated that going forward I needed to turn my head to the right to swallow without choking. 2022 my quality of life began the downhill spiral, with falling, using handrails at Sue's house, a wheelchair to go out, soft foods and thickened liquid drinks. I continued under Hospice care, which all my nurses were truly kind. The highlight of my week was receiving music therapy with Sadie. She would bring her violin to play just for my enjoyment. Mostly she tried to get me to sing along with her while she played favorite songs on her guitar. Also, a great delight for me was my visits with Chaplain Edward. His word for me from the Word of God and his prayers prayed for me blessed my life. The care I received from all the workers at Vitas was exceptional.

Linda came to Sue's house from Thailand to spend several weeks with me during the holidays of Thanksgiving and Christmas. She stayed until after New Year so Sue could have time off with her family. She returned early to Thailand as John had to have his heart shocked back into rhythm. Thankfully, their daughter Katie flew up to be with her dad in Chiang Rai for this procedure. Grateful to God that the procedure was successful.

February 3, 2023, I enter an assistant living facility, The Reserve in Woodstock, Georgia, less than five miles from Sue's home. I had a choking episode that Sue was unable to help me resolve, and we decided it was time for me to get more help. I also had fallen a couple of times in my bedroom, finally realizing it was the slide-on slippers causing me to trip. We all thought this was going to be a temporary visit to assisted living as plans were for me to go and stay with Linda and John once they were back in Florida for their short furlough. However, it was more temporary than any of us ever thought.

Thirteen days later Hospice was called in for my final days here on earth. Sue and Michael came to sit with me, and Jeremiah and his sons came to say their goodbyes. I had been unresponsive until I heard Jeremiah's voice. I opened my eyes and Sue said to me, "you hear Jeremiah, don't you?" I nodded, closed my eyes never to open them again. The Hospice nurse told Sue that I could last from four to seven days in this condition and to go home and get a little sleep. Sue woke up at 3 a.m. as was her custom to give me medicine and her phone was lit up with the Hospice nurse calling to say, "I'm sorry, but she's gone." Sue and Michael rushed over to the facility and stayed with my body until the Hospice nurse who could pronounce me deceased arrived. She pronounced me dead at 5:01 a.m. but I was already in Heaven.

God answered all our prayers as I had desired to just go to sleep and wake up in Heaven, Linda prayed that I would not have a traumatic death with another stroke or falling down Sue's multiple stairs. Sue prayed knowing that my time was near for me to not linger.

*You can't change the past, but you can choose to think differently and change your future.*

Obituary: Lila Cox, Mother, Wife, Nana, Gigi, Triple G, Spiritual Mom to many died peacefully in her sleep on February 16, 2023, in Woodstock, Georgia. She is predeceased in death by her parents, James and May Moore, her loving husband of almost

50 years Rex Cox, her siblings, Arad Moore, Nellie Moore, Thelma Adele Smith, Marvin Moore, and Robert Moore, and great-grandson Daniel Echols.

Lila is survived by her two daughters, Sue Schultz (husband Michael) and Linda Gibson (husband John); four grandchildren Jeremiah Schultz, Gracie Echols, Kimberly Gibson Tran, and Kaitlyn Huhmann; five great-grandchildren Nathan Echols, Jonathan Schultz, Jewel Echols, Brianna Echols, and Jonah Schultz; and one great-great granddaughter Izzy Echols.

Lila took her job seriously to stay home and raise her daughters. When she became a grandmother, she promised to be the best Nana she could as her grandparents had died before she could know them.

Lila worked in bookkeeping and accounting until age 80, finally retiring from the International Mission Board where she ministered in Jesus' Name in England, Thailand, and other Asian countries.

Lila's greatest joy was helping people to know and love her Lord Jesus, who was the Anchor for her soul.

Now finally Home, dancing in the brilliant fields of Grace!

Printed in the United States
by Baker & Taylor Publisher Services